ZOLLGRENZSCHUTZ

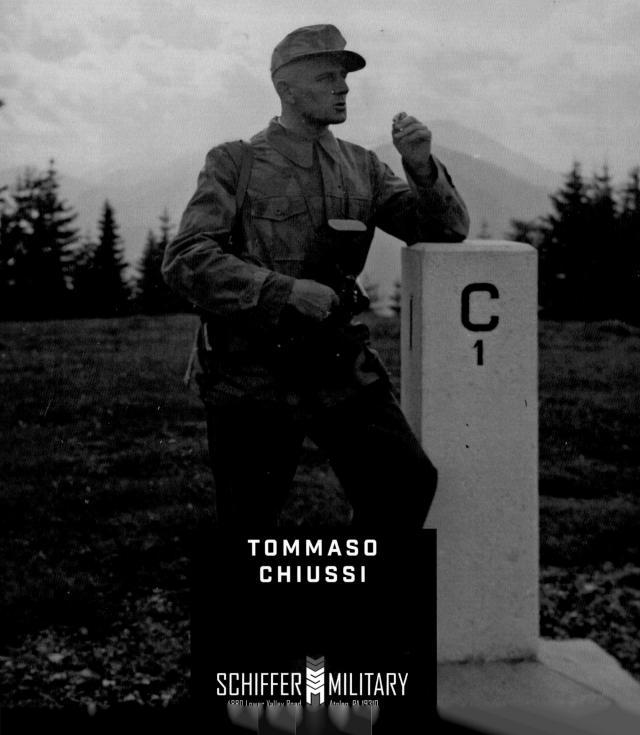

ZOLLGRENZSCHUTZ

Border Guards on the Frontier of the Reich,
Hauptzollamt Villach, 1941–1945

**TOMMASO
CHIUSSI**

SCHIFFER MILITARY
4880 Lower Valley Road · Atglen, PA 19310

Other Schiffer books by the author

Globocnik's Men in Italy, 1943–45: Abteilung R and the SS-Wachmannschaften of the Operationszone Adriatisches Küstenland,

Stefano Di Giusto & Tommaso Chiussi, ISBN 978-0-7643-5254-6

Other Schiffer books on related subjects

Police Battalions of the Third Reich,

Stephen Campbell, ISBN 978-0-7643-2771-1

Combat Operations of the German Ordnungspolizei, 1939–1945: Polizei-Bataillone • SS-Polizei-Regimenter,

Rolf Michaelis, ISBN 978-0-7643-3659-1

Designed by Christopher Bower
Cover design by Christopher Bower
Type set in Industry/Minion Pro

ISBN: 978-0-7643-6705-2
Printed in China

Published by Schiffer Publishing, Ltd.
4880 Lower Valley Road
Atglen, PA 19310
Phone: (610) 593-1777; Fax: (610) 593-2002
Email: Info@schifferbooks.com
Web: www.schifferbooks.com

For our complete selection of fine books on this and related subjects, please visit our website at www.schifferbooks.com. You may also write for a free catalog.

Schiffer Publishing's titles are available at special discounts for bulk purchases for sales promotions or premiums. Special editions, including personalized covers, corporate imprints, and excerpts, can be created in large quantities for special needs. For more information, contact the publisher.

We are always looking for people to write books on new and related subjects. If you have an idea for a book, please contact us at proposals@schifferbooks.com.

FSC
www.fsc.org
MIX
Paper from
responsible sources
FSC® C167893

Dedication

To my ancestors

Acknowledgments

I would like to thank the following persons who have contributed to the research: Albert Smetanin, Blaž Torkar, Ernst Seidl, Eugenio Vendrame, Gerard Kenny, Gianfranco Ciuffarin, Guido Ronconi, Ian Jewison, Jürgen Wagner, Kevin Jacobs, Marcello Ravaioli, Marko Vidmar, Martin Premk, Michael Mair, Rainer Schütz, Raphael Riccio, Rene Duschl, Roberto Fontana, Saso Skok, Stefano Commentucci, Stefano Di Giusto, Stéphane Pauli, Stephen Tyas, Susan Köhnke, Uroš Košir, Wilhelm Saris, Alfred Uranšek (Zollwachemuseum Bleiburg), Damjana Fortunat Černilogar (Tolminski Muzej), Dr. David Hamann (Research & Transcription Service Berlin), Saša Mesec and Špela Spolej Milat (Slovenski Planinski Muzej), Martin Achrainer (Historisches Archiv Österreichischer Alpenverein), Gorenjski muzej Kranj, Ing. Monika Tschofenig-Hebein (Marktgemeinde Arnoldstein), Ernst Wiegele, and Mag. Thomas Zeloth, Irene Kerschbaumer, and Udo Kampl (Kärntner Landesarchiv). Last, a special thanks goes to Detlev Zuckarelli, Elia Di Fonzo, Luca Cossa, and Marcus Schreiner-Božič, without whose help this study could not have seen the light.

Consultants: Darko Cafuta and Klemen Kocjančič for the Slovenian archives and sources, Grega Žorž for the history of the "Rapallo border," and Marc Goris for the organizational structure of the Zollgrenzschutz.

Contents

Introduction

Since the end of World War II, probably due to their "civilian" origins, the units of the Zollgrenzschutz and Verstärkter Grenzaufsichtsdienst have rarely attracted the attention of scholars and military history enthusiasts. Except for some noteworthy insights, such as the works of Walter Eulitz, Wilhelm Saris, and Detlev Zuckarelli, publications dedicated to this topic are uncommon and often characterized by a low level of detail. An in-depth study instead seems necessary, since it shows how these units, formed by civilian "militarized" staff, played a role of primary importance within the German war machine, being not infrequently employed in highly dangerous contexts such as the antipartisan operations. The reconstruction of the command structure and the events regarding the units analyzed in this study proved to be particularly difficult, mainly due to an almost total lack of contemporaneous documentation. Furthermore, events and organizational structures are often described in reports written by the members of these units in unclear terms, which has undoubtedly contributed to obscuring the general picture. This unclarity was probably caused by the personnel's "civilian" origin, and hence their limited familiarity with regulations and standardizations typical of the military world, as well as by insufficient personnel training, especially for what concerns the last years of the war.

The surviving documentation related to the Hauptzollamt Villach is undoubtedly very scarce. In fact, with the exception of a paperwork collection originating from the archive of the Bezirkszollkommissariat (G) Wocheiner-Feistritz, kept at the Arhiv Republike Slovenije in Ljubljana (archive collection SI AS 2175, tehnične enota 17), and of a fair number of personal files and two captioned photo albums preserved at the Kärntner Landesarchiv in Klagenfurt (archive collections AT-KLA 39-C-18 and AT-KLA 128-F-H 61), there are no other organic collections of material known on this theme. Regarding the personal files kept at the Österreiches Staatsarchiv in Vienna (archive collection AT-OeStA / AdR MilEv ZGS) and at the Steiermark Landesarchiv in Graz (noninventoried fund), their consultation has been made difficult due to the privacy regulations to which they are in part currently subjected. For the reasons set out above, it is certainly likely that the reconstruction of the organizational structures and events reported in the text, which was in some cases made possible only by relying on hypotheses or speculations, is susceptible to future additions or corrections based on the consultation of the documentation currently not available or not yet discovered.

The illustrations presented in support of this study deserve a separate mention. This comes mainly from two distinct photographic groups relating to Zollgrenzschutz units subordinated to the Hauptzollamt Villach. The first one, currently part of the author's archive, is made up of about twenty photos that, on the basis of the captions written on the back of some of them, would seem to originate from the belongings of Zollinspektor Kellerer. Later promoted to *Oberzollinspektor*, Kellerer was initially Bezirkszollkommissar (G) Wocheiner-Feistritz and later, it seems, for a short time, also Bezirkszollkommissar (G) Kronau. The second group, currently kept at the Kärntner Landesarchiv of Klagenfurt (archive collection AT-KLA 128-F-H 61), consists of two photo albums assembled after the war by Zollsekretär Karl Pfister. Later promoted to *Oberzollsekretär*, Pfister was initially *Postenführer* of the Grenzaufsichtsstelle Kronau and later *Beamte zur besonderen Verwendung* at the Bezirkszollkommissariat (G) Kronau. Noteworthy is the fact that some of the photographs contained in these two albums, taken by Pfister himself during the war, are also present in the Kellerer group.

Notes for the reader

Throughout the text, towns and villages that were inside the German or Italian borders at the time of the events and are now in Slovenia are called with their current name. A list with the corresponding former German or Italian names is provided at the end of the book.

The German designations of the Alpine huts and the Zollgrenzschutz outposts / altitude outposts mentioned in the text were not always clear, or they varied significantly during the years. For this reason in some cases such denominations are only speculative.

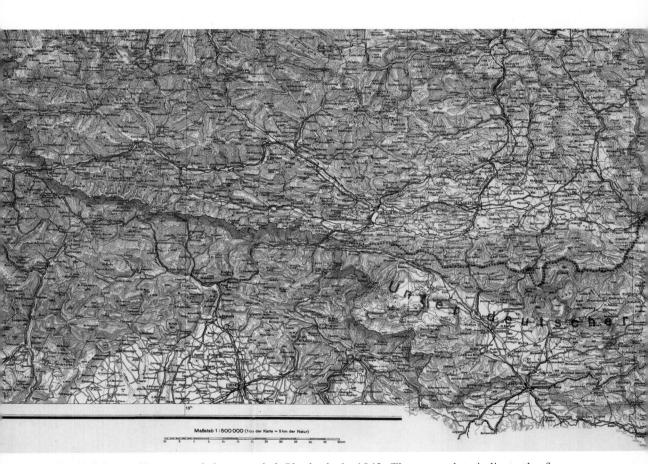

The Reichsgau Kärnten and the occupied Oberkrain in 1943. The green dots indicate the former "Karawankengrenze"/"*Polizeigrenze.*"

CHAPTER 1
The Zollgrenzschutz-Verstärkter Grenzaufsichtsdienst

Over the 1930s–1940s, as in most of the other European nations, the Deutsches Reich (Hitler's Germany) also raised its own border protection units or border guard. Since 1937, the Reichsgrenze (Reich's border) protection and control were ensured by the Zollgrenzschutz (customs-border protection), which was a uniformed civilian corps formed by customs personnel subordinated to the *Reichsminister der Finanzen* (Reich's finance minister) within the Reichsfinanzverwaltung (Reich's Finance Administration).[1] In the case of conflict with a neighboring country, the German military authorities could mobilize the Verstärkter Grenzaufsichtsdienst (VGAD, reinforced border control service), which consisted of Zollgrenzschutz members, additional customs officers, and military-trained civilians living in areas near the Reichsgrenze. For this reason, during World War II the Zollgrenzschutz and the VGAD terms were used more and more in parallel, becoming essentially synonymous.[2]

In the German regions along the Reichsgrenze, the *Reichsminister der Finanzen* delegated the border protection and control to the *Oberfinanzpräsidium mit Grenze* (higher finance offices with border),[3] which were led by an *Oberfinanzpräsident* (president of the Oberfinanzpräsidium).

The *Oberfinanzpräsident* in turn delegated this task to subordinated departments known as *Hauptzollamt* (G) (HZA, main customs offices with border), which were led by *Vorsteher des Hauptzollamts* (directors of the HZA). In addition to controlling the Zollgrenzschutz units and ensuring border protection, the HZA were also in charge of tax and customs matters. In the *besetztes Gebiet* (occupied territories) or in the areas subjected to the German army's administration, the Zollgrenzschutz was required to carry out its tasks under the orders of the military authorities. Therefore, in the occupied regions the Zollgrenzschutz became basically a military corps, although it still belonged to the Reichsfinanzverwaltung and, by order of the military authorities, took over the border protection. In order to avoid giving the impression that the Reichsfinanzministerium (Reich's Finance Ministry) had taken over the finance administration in occupied territories and to point out the subordination to the military authorities, in these areas the HZA designation was replaced by the more military-sounding term of *Befehlsstelle des Zollgrenzschutzes* (BefSt des Zollgrenzschutzes, Zollgrenzschutz headquarters), led by the Leiter der Befehlsstelle des Zollgrenzschutzes (heads of the BefSt des Zollgrenzschutzes). As to the occupied territories that were considered historically as being part of "Großdeutschland"—such as, for example, Sudetenland, Elsass, Luxemburg, and Oberkrain/Untersteiermark, as soon as they were officially annexed to the Reich or became subjected to German civilian administration, the local Reichsfinanzverwaltung organization went back to its usual HZA network. During the last months of the war, when military matters became more and more important, some of these HZA were renamed BefSt des Zollgrenzschutzes as they became part again of the military structures. On the other hand, in the occupied areas that were not considered part of the Deutsches Reich—such as, for example, the Generalgouvernement, the Netherlands, Ukraine, and Serbia—the organizational structure of the BefSt des Zollgrenzschutzes was kept during the entire war, no matter whether there was a German civilian or military administration in place. Also in the latter areas, from 1941 onward, offices known as *Hauptbefehlsstelle* and *Kommandostelle* (main headquarters and command posts) were elected as superior authority to the BefSt des Zollgrenzschutzes; they centrally commanded and coordinated the Zollgrenzschutz and acted as a main contact for military and civil authorities. In military terms, the HZA / BefSt des Zollgrenzschutzes served substantially as operational higher commands and made use of the Zollgrenzschutz units subordinated to them.

Each *Oberfinanzpräsidium* (G) had, within their own structure, an *Abteilung Zoll* (customs office), to which was directly subordinated the Grenzreferat (department for the borders matters). This department, led by the *Grenzreferent* (head of the Grenzreferat), was responsible for all border-related issues of technical and legal character, as well as for organizational issues related to the Zollgrenzschutz units based in its area of responsibility. The *Grenzreferent* worked closely together with the Vorsteher des HZA / Leiter der BefSt des Zollgrenzschutzes in relation to all the abovementioned matters. Furthermore, from 1943 onward, within the *Abteilung Zoll* of each *Oberfinanzpräsidium* (G), a Gruppe für Zollgrenzschutz or Zollgrenzschutz-Referat (Zollgrenzschutz department) was created, on which information is very scarce.

For the "in the field" border control, the HZA relied on the *Bezirkszollkommissar* (G) (BZKom [G], chiefs of the district customs commissariats with border), each in charge of a *Bezirkszollkommissariat* (G) (also abbreviated as BZKom [G], district customs commissariats with border). The BZKom (G), which in military terms basically acted as *Stab* (unit's headquarters), carried out the military and civilian tasks assigned to the Zollgrenzschutz. With regard to the civilian tasks, the BZKom (G) was the highest representative of the Zollgrenzschutz near the border, and besides the administrative work, its main responsibility was to control the posts known as *Grenzaufsichtsstelle/Zollaufsichtsstelle* (G), to ensure the efficiency of the border protection, and, in some cases, to deal with disciplinary matters among its border guards. The territory subordinated to the jurisdiction of a BZKom (G) was commonly known as *Dienstbereich* or *Dienstbezirk* (sector of duty), which included a specific border section, indicated as *Grenzabschnitt*.[4]

For the "in the field" border control of the assigned *Grenzabschnitt* and for the collection of the customs duties inside its own *Dienstbereich*, every BZKom (G) relied, in peacetime, on a network of *Zollaufsichtsstelle* (G) (ZASt [G], customs inspection posts with border), later renamed *Grenzaufsichtsstelle* (GASt, border control posts).[5] In command of a GASt/ZASt (G) was usually an *Aufsichtsführender Beamter* (supervisory officer); this position was often simply indicated as *Postenführer* (post commander). To such posts were directly subordinated the *Stützpunkt/Höhenstützpunkt* (outposts / altitude outposts), based in locations considered particularly important or sensitive.

Part of the organizational structure of the HZA were also the *Zollamt* (G) (customs suboffices with border), which were considered as *Hilfsstelle des Hauptzollamts* (help departments of the HZA), while the *Zollamt* (G) I were directly subordinated to the HZA, due to factors of different nature (size, location, traffic, importance, etc.), the Zollamt (G) II and III were in some cases also directly subordinated to the BZKom (G). When one of these suboffices was located at or next to a border crossing, it was generically referred to as a *Grenzzollstelle* (border-crossing customs department); when it was based on a *Landstrasse*, it was indicated as a *Landstraßenzollamt* or *Straßenzollamt* (state roads customs suboffice); and when based at a railway station, it was known as an *Eisenbahnzollamt* (railway customs suboffice).

Finally, subordinated to the BZKom (G) were also the personnel seconded to the *Grenzübergangsstelle* (border-crossing checkpoints).

The generic term used by the competent authorities to refer to all these offices was *Dienststelle des Zollgrenzschutzes* (Zollgrenzschutz duty departments), or, more rarely, *Zolldienststelle an der Grenze* (customs duty departments at the border). The monitoring of the activities of all those *Dienststelle* was ensured by the *Generalinspekteur des Zollgrenzschutzes* (Zollgrenzschutz general inspectorate), who was directly subordinated, via the *Staatssekretär*'s office, to the Reichsfinanzministerium.

As a consequence of the attempted assassination of Hitler on July 20, 1944, the Zollgrenzschutz was subordinated to the *Reichsführer-SS*, Heinrich Himmler, who took control over it in quality of Chef der Sicherheitspolizei und des SD,[6] via the Generalgrenzinspekteur (the border general inspectorate). His project, later only partially completed, was to gather the Zollgrenzschutz-VGAD and the Grenzpolizei in one entity, called Grenzschutzkorps, within the newly established Gruppe IV G (Dienststelle des Generalgrenzinspekteurs) of the Reichssicherheitshauptamt.[7]

CHAPTER 2
The Reichsgrenze in the Kreis Villach and Radmannsdorf

The southern boundary of the Kreis Villach (territorial district of Villach), at the time part of the Reichsgau Kärnten (Carinthia region, Austria), coincided, until 1941, with the line of the Reichsgrenze, which ran, along the Carnic Alps and the Karavanke mountain range, on the line Oisternig (Ostgipfel)–border crossing of Coccau/Thörl–Ofen–Wurzenpass–Mallestiger Mittagskogel–Mittagskogel–Frauenkogel–Kahlkogel–Kotschnasattel, essentially following the current Austrian border with Italy and Slovenia.

After the dissolution of the Kingdom of Yugoslavia in the spring of 1941, vast territories of the current northern Slovenia, including the Štajerska and Gorenjska regions, were annexed to the Reich. The Štajerska was aggregated to the Reichsgau Steiermark (Styria region, Austria) with the name of Untersteiermark (Lower Styria). The Gorenjska was attached to the Reichsgau Kärnten, initially with the name Süd-Kärnten (Southern Carinthia) and then, from early 1942, with the one of Oberkrain (Upper Carniola) and was subdivided in the Kreis Krainburg (Kranj), Radmannsdorf (Radovljica), and Stein in Oberkrain (Kamnik). The Oberkrain was subordinated to the Zivilverwaltung in den besetzten Gebieten Kärntens und Krains (civilian administration for the occupied territories of Carinthia and Carniola), led since the end of 1941 by the *Gauleiter* of the Reichsgau Kärnten, SS-Obergruppenführer Friedrich Rainer, with headquarters in Klagenfurt (Kreis Klagenfurt). The Reichsgau Kärnten and Steiermark, together with all the occupied territories attached to them, were placed under the territorial jurisdiction of the Höherer SS- und Polizeiführer im Wehrkreis XVIII (HSSPF im Wehrkreis XVIII, higher commander of the SS/Polizei in the XVIII military district, formerly known as SS-Oberabschnitt Alpenland), a position occupied since December 1941 by SS-Obergruppenführer und Generalleutnant der Polizei Erwin Rösener. The headquarters of this command were initially based in Salzburg (Reichsgau Salzburg), later in Bled (Kreis Radmannsdorf), and last in Ljubljana (Provinz Laibach).

Following the creation of the Oberkrain, the so-called "Karawankengrenze"—that is, the Reichsgrenze running along the Karavanke mountains—was moved southwest, along the recently dissolved former Italian-Yugoslav frontier, also known as the "Rapallo border."[1] From 1941, therefore, the line of the Reichsgrenze in the Kreis Villach was reduced to the mountain stretch Oisternig (Ostgipfel)–border crossing of Coccau/Thörl–Ofen (also known as Peč or Monte Forno). The next stretch followed the western boundary of the newly created Kreis Radmannsdorf, settling on the mountain line Ofen–border crossing of Fusine/Rateče–Visoka Ponca (or Ponza Grande)–V Koncu špica (or Monte Termine)–Jalovec–Prelaz Vršič–Prisojnik–Razor–Triglav–Kanjavec–Velika Vrata–Lanževica–Bogatinsko sedlo–Tolminski Kuk–Vogel–Rodica–Črna prst–Možic/Bohinjsko sedlo, essentially cutting across the entire chain of the Julian Alps. Between the Bohinjsko sedlo (a pass known to Italians as Sella Bochinisa) and the border crossing of Soriška Planina, the line of the Reichsgrenze continued into the Kreis Krainburg. In the Kreis Radmannsdorf, the new Reichsgrenze bordered with two provinces of the Regno d'Italia (Kingdom of Italy): the Provincia di Udine (Udine Province, in the stretch Ofen–V Koncu špica) and the Provincia di Gorizia (Gorizia Province, in the stretch V Koncu špica–Možic/Bohinjsko sedlo).[2]

Following the Italian armistice of September 8, 1943, the Italian provinces of Fiume, Gorizia, Pola, Trieste, Udine, and Lubiana were incorporated by the Germans in a region called Operationszone Adriatisches Küstenland (OZAK, Adriatic Littoral operations area), placed under Rainer's civilian administration in anticipation of a future annexation to the Reich. The provinces of Fiume, Gorizia, Pola, Trieste, and Udine fell under the jurisdiction of the Höherer SS- und Polizeiführer Adriatisches Küstenland (higher commander of the SS/Polizei in the OZAK), SS-Gruppenführer und Generalleutnant der Polizei Odilo Globocnik, while Lubiana Province (called Provinz Laibach by the Germans) was subordinated to Rösener. In this context, therefore, this section of the Reichsgrenze separated territories that were under German civilian administration on both sides of the border.[3]

Slovenian sector of the Julian Alps, 1943–44. Zollsekretär Karl Pfister, *Postenführer* of GASt Kronau, apparently climbing in the area between Mounts Prisojnik and Razor; in the background are the localities of Krnica and Mala Pišnica. © *Kärntner Landesarchiv*

Slovenian sector of the Julian Alps, 1943–44. Zollsekretär Pfister and one of his men on the top of Mount Jalovec; in the background is the Mangart massif. The Reichsgrenze ran between these two mountains.
© *Kärntner Landesarchiv*

Slovenian sector of the Julian Alps, 1943–44. Zollsekretär Pfister (*on the left*), near the border stone 7/XXIX, on the top of Mount Prisojnik. © *Kärntner Landesarchiv*

Zollsekretär Pfister (*in the foreground*) having fun with his men and some civilians in the "Stube," likely in Kranjska Gora (Slovenia), 1944–45. © *Kärntner Landesarchiv*

Slovenian sector of the Julian Alps, 1943–44. Zollsekretär Pfister posing in front of the massif of Mount Triglav, 1943–44. © *Kärntner Landesarchiv*

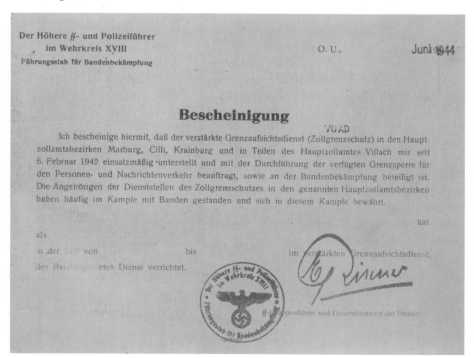

Der Höhere ⚡- und Polizeiführer
im Wehrkreis XVIII   O. U.,   Juni 1944
Führungsstab für Bandenbekämpfung

Bescheinigung

VGAD

Ich bescheinige hiermit, daß der verstärkte Grenzaufsichtsdienst (Zollgrenzschutz) in den Hauptzollamtsbezirken Marburg, Cilli, Krainburg und in Teilen des Hauptzollamtes Villach mir seit 6. Februar 1942 einsatzmäßig unterstellt und mit der Durchführung der verfügten Grenzsperre für den Personen- und Nachrichtenverkehr beauftragt, sowie an der Bandenbekämpfung beteiligt ist. Die Angehörigen der Dienststellen des Zollgrenzschutzes in den genannten Hauptzollamtsbezirken haben häufig im Kampfe mit Banden gestanden und sich in diesem Kampfe bewährt.

                                                                                                        hat

als

in der Zeit von   bis   im verstärkten Grenzaufsichtsdienst

des Bandengebietes Dienst verrichtet.

                                                                        ⚡-...penführer und Generalleutnant der Polizei

CHAPTER 3
The Organizational Structure of the Hauptzollamt Villach (Oberfinanzpräsidium Graz), 1941–1945

As mentioned, security in the Reichsgau Kärnten and Steiermark and in the occupied territories attached to them fell under the jurisdiction of the HSSPF im Wehrkreis XVIII. Due to the importance of these regions for access to the Balkans, from late 1941, Rösener was given the responsibility for the fight against the partisan movement, which was particularly active in the area. For this reason, all units based in the areas subject to Rösener that were in charge of security matters, including the Zollgrenzschutz personnel of the HZA Villach, were subordinated to the HSSPF im Wehrkreis XVIII. For accomplishing these tasks, Rösener initially made use of the Befehlshaber der Ordnungspolizei Alpenland (BdO Alpenland, commander of the Order Police Alpenland), and later of the purposely created Führungsstab für Bandenbekämpfung (central command for the fight against partisan bands). Given the critical situation caused by partisan activity, in June 1943 Himmler declared Oberkrain as *Bandenkampfgebiet* (territory of fight against the partisan bands); also, in order to improve the control over its territory, this region was declared as a *Schutzgebiet* (protected area) and, in 1944, was subdivided into *Sicherungsabschnitt* (security sectors), each assigned to a *Kommandant des Sicherungsabschnittes* (commander of the Sicherungsabschnitt). The same thing also was apparently applied to the southern part of the Kreis Klagenfurt and Villach, but information in this regard remains vague. In case of emergency, the units of the Zollgrenzschutz were placed under the operational control of the *Kommandant des Sicherungsabschnittes*, which basically acted as representatives of Rösener within their own Sicherungsabschnitt.[1]

The control and the protection of the Reichsgrenze in these areas fell under the responsibility of the Oberfinanzpräsidium Graz, which was created in June 1938 and was based in Graz (Reichsgau Steiermark). The position of Oberfinanzpräsident Graz was held by Dr. Richard Richter, whose headquarters was at Palais Meran in Leonhardstrasse nr. 15 (now Kunstuniversität Graz); *Vertreter* (deputy) of Richter in this office was, from early 1939 to mid-1942, Finanzpräsident Walter Jungk and later Regierungsdirektor Dr. Alexander Rödling. Based at the same address was the Abteilung Personal und Verwaltung (Staff and Administration Department) of the Oberfinanzpräsidium Graz, also referred to as (P), initially directed by Richter himself and later by Regierungsdirektor Roßmüller. The Abteilung Steuer and Abteilung Zoll (Taxes and Customs Departments) were located at Conrad von Hötzendorf-Strasse nr. 14–18. The Abteilung Steuer, also referred to as (St), was led between late 1938 and early 1943 by Finanzpräsident Dr. Franz Schön and later by Finanzpräsident Fuchs; deputy in this department, at least in 1941–1943, was Regierungsdirektor Hirsch. Director of the Abteilung Zoll, also referred to as (Z), was, from early 1941 to early 1942, Regierungsrat Dr. Berroth; until mid-1942, Finanzpräsident Jungk; and from late 1942, Finanzpräsident Dr. Rödling. Deputy in this department in 1941–1942 was Regierungsdirektor Dr. Rainer, and in 1943, Regierungsdirektor Dr. Andreas Strametz, an officer active at the Oberfinanzpräsidium Graz since late 1939. As to the Grenzreferat Graz department, which was based in Conrad von Hötzendorf-Strasse nr. 14–18 too, information is scarce. At least from 1944, but possibly also during the previous years, the Grenzreferat Graz department was certainly led by Oberregierungsrat Dr. Friedrich Sperling, who had belonged to the Abteilung Zoll of the Oberfinanzpräsidium Graz since 1940; between June and September 1944, Sperling was apparently replaced by Oberregierungsrat Robert Spieß. It is also known that in 1943, the Gruppe für Zollgrenzschutz within the Abteilung Zoll was led by Finanzpräsident Dr. Rödling, while his deputy was Regierungsdirektor Dr. Strametz.

Since 1939–1940, subordinated to the Oberfinanzpräsidium Graz were the HZA Fürstenfeld, Graz, Graz-Grenze, and Leoben, based in the Reichsgau Steiermark, and the HZA Lienz, Klagenfurt, and Villach, based in the Reichsgau Kärnten. From April 1941, following the occupation of northern Slovenia by the German army, created and subordinated to the Oberfinanzpräsidium Graz were also the BefSt des Zollgrenzschutzes Krainburg, based in Kranj in the Gorenjska (shortly thereafter named Oberkrain), Cilli, and Marburg an der Drau, respectively located in Celje and Maribor in the Štajerska (shortly thereafter named Untersteiermark). During the following October, the BefSt des Zollgrenzschutzes Krainburg, Cilli, and Marburg an der Drau also changed their designation to HZA. Furthermore, following the Italian armistice of September 1943, the BefSt des Zollgrenzschutzes Laibach, created in the former Provincia di Lubiana, recently subordinated to Rösener with the name of Provinz Laibach, was also subordinated to the Oberfinanzpräsidium Graz. Last, apparently in early 1945, a BefSt des Zollgrenzschutzes Arch was active; it was based at the castle of the village of Raka (Untersteiermark), but nothing is known about its direct subordination.

The HZA Villach was officially created in May 1939, although the Reichsfinanzverwaltung had made use of the existing organizational structures of the former Austrian finance administration since 1938. During 1939, its offices were located in Villach in Pestalozzistrasse nr. 24, to be transferred later to 10. Oktoberstrasse nr. 11. At least from May 1942 the position of Vorsteher des HZA Villach was occupied by Regierungsrat Dr. Hans-Joachim Rathke,[2] who was replaced in this function in May 1943 by Zollrat Dr. Rapf, previously serving at the Zollamt Brenner-Bahnhof (HZA Innsbruck) and at the HZA Fürstenfeld. It seems that at least between late 1941 and mid-1944, Oberzollinspektor Richard Siedle held the position of deputy of the Vorsteher des HZA Villach. From mid-September 1943, an officer indicated as BZKom (G) Friedrich Gebhardt apparently acted as adjutant of Rapf at the HZA Villach; he kept this position continuously until the office was disbanded. From 1941, the HZA Villach exercised its authority over the Reichsgrenze along the mountain line Oisternig (Ostgipfel)–Ofen in the Kreis Villach, and along the Ofen-Možic / Bohinjsko sedlo line in the Kreis Radmannsdorf. The HZA Villach jurisdiction bordered in the southeast with the Kreis Krainburg, a district subordinated to the HZA Krainburg, which was based in Kranj/Stražišče (Kreis Krainburg); the position of Vorsteher des HZA Krainburg was held, at least from the summer of 1942, by Regierungsrat Edmund Ernst, previously Vorsteher des HZA Klagenfurt, who later fell in action, apparently on the Eastern Front. Ernst was replaced, at least from July 1943, by Zollrat Hahn, coming from the BefSt des Zollgrenzschutzes Stryj (Distrikt Galizien), and was later promoted to Regierungsrat. Since the autumn of 1943, perhaps as a consequence of the Italian armistice, the HZA Villach authority was extended to the southeast, apparently as far as the border crossing of Slugov grič (northeast of Cerkno), effectively extending its own jurisdiction over a short stretch of the Reichsgrenze previously subordinated to the HZA Krainburg. To the northwest, the HZA Villach jurisdiction bordered with the Kreis Hermagor, a district subordinated to the HZA Lienz, which was based in Lienz (Kreis Lienz); the position of Vorsteher des HZA Lienz was initially held by Zollrat Chaselon and, at least from early 1944, by Zollrat Köster.[3]

As mentioned, during the summer of 1944 the Zollgrenzschutz was subordinated to Himmler, through the *Generalgrenzinspekteur*, based within the Reichssicherheitshauptamt. As a consequence of this change, from the following autumn, the Grenzreferat Graz was integrated into the Referat IV G of the Befehlshaber der Sipo/SD in Salzburg (BdS Salzburg, commander of the Sipo/SD of Salzburg).[4] Therefore, from early October, Oberregierungsrat Sperling held the position of *Grenzreferent* at the BdS Salzburg, while keeping his office in Conrad von Hötzendorf-Strasse nr. 14–18 in Graz; deputy of Sperling, at least from November 1944 to January 1945, was Oberzollinspektor Eugen Katz. In addition, in late 1944, Sperling created within its own office in Graz two subordinated positions indicated as Grenzreferent für Steiermark und Untersteiermark and Grenzreferent für Kärnten und Oberkrain. The tasks of these new sections remain unclear; however, it is reasonable to assume that, given the extension of the territory assigned to the responsibilities of the *Grenzreferat* of the BdS Salzburg in Graz, Sperling had created them in order to split his tasks and lighten his workload. Nothing is known about the activities of these two sections, except that in November 1944 the position of Grenzreferent für Steiermark und Untersteiermark was held by Sperling himself. According to some uclear information, the position of Grenzreferent für Kärnten und Oberkrain was occupied by Oberregierungsrat Robert Spieß. Furthermore, since October–November 1944, at least another Grenzreferat department, based in Salzburg, was created within the structure of the BdS Salzburg. Nothing is known about the activities and the subordination of this office. The only information available comes from some reports, forwarded in late 1944- early 1945 by the Vorsteher des HZA Krainburg and Villach and by Sperling—as Grenzreferent of the BdS Salzburg in Graz—to the "Grenzreferenten in Salzburg." Oberregierungsrat Spieß may have referred to this department when he declared that from late September 1944 to late April 1945, he had held the unspecified position of "Grenzreferent des BdS Salzburg" apparently in Salzburg. However, it is not clear if, at this point, the Grenzreferat des BdS Salzburg in Salzburg and the Grenzreferat für Kärnten und Oberkrain were actually the very same office.

As a consequence of these events and in view of further changes, during the autumn of 1944 the HZA Krainburg and Villach changed their names to BefSt des Zollgrenzschutzes, while remaining under the command, respectively, of Regierungsrat Hahn and Zollrat Rapf. Furthermore, in late 1944–early 1945, at the initiative of the *Grenzreferent* of the BdS Salzburg in Graz, four border guard departments were set up, indicated as Abteilung Zollgrenzschutz Kärnten in Lienz, Oberkrain in Krainburg, Steiermark in Fürstenfeld, and Untersteiermark in Cilli. All these departments were to be formed with the Zollgrenzschutz forces previously subordinated to the Oberfinanzpräsidium Graz, apparently within the IV G office of their respective local centers of the Gestapo; it remains unclear which was the correct designation of the latter offices, since the only information known in this regard comes from a report sent by Sperling in early 1945 to an office called "Staatspolizeistelle Graz-Abtl. IV G." This meant that from that moment on, the border guards active in the area were organized and employed according to the territorial organization of the BdS Salzburg. For this reason, at that stage, the BefSt des Zollgrenzschutzes Villach found itself in a very peculiar position. As seen already, its border guards were deployed both in the proper Reichsgau Kärnten and in the occupied Oberkrain, whose territories were subordinated to two different jurisdictions of the BdS Salzburg: in late 1944, the Kreis Villach was under the Staatspolizeileitstelle Klagenfurt (Gestapo regional headquarters of Klagenfurt), while the Kreis Krainburg and Radmannsdorf were under the Kommandeur der Sipo/SD in den besetzten Gebieten Kärntens und Krains in Veldes (KdS Veldes, commander of the Sipo/SD of Bled). Therefore, in consequence of Sperling's order, the border guards of the BefSt des Zollgrenzschutzes Villach active in the Kreis Villach came to be subordinated—through the Abteilung Zollgrenzschutz Kärnten in Lienz—to the Staatspolizeileitstelle Klagenfurt, while those based in the Kreis Krainburg and Radmannsdorf—through the Abteilung Zollgrenzschutz Oberkrain in Krainburg—to the KdS Veldes.

Information about the Abteilung Zollgrenzschutz Oberkrain in Krainburg is fragmentary; according to the available documentation, this department, based in Kranj/Stražišče (Kreis Krainburg), was established on the basis of the BefSt des Zollgrenzschutzes Krainburg, apparently as part of the IV G office, within the KdS Veldes. In any case, during 1945 this department—sometimes also indicated as "Abt. Zollgrenzschutz Oberkrain-Hauptzollamt"—kept using the stamps of the HZA Krainburg / BefSt des Zollgrenzschutzes Krainburg. *Leiter* of the Abteilung Zollgrenzschutz Oberkrain in Krainburg was Regierungsrat Hahn.[5] His adjutant or deputy might have been Regierungsrat Enderlein, previously BZKom (G) Laak-West (HZA Krainburg); Oberzollsekretär Hannawald and an officer named Schmid also worked very closely with Hahn in this department. In early April 1945, the Abteilung Zollgrenzschutz Oberkrain in Krainburg was moved to Bled (Kreis Radmannsdorf), probably basing at the headquarters of the KdS Veldes; between late April and early May was also active, within the latter office, a Grenzreferat department on which nothing is known except that it was led by Oberregierungsrat Robert Spieß. According to very uncertain data, it seems that in March 1945, the BZKom (G) St. Martin, Littai (both in the Kreis Stein in Oberkrain), St. Veit, Laak-Süd, Laak-West (all in the Kreis Krainburg), and Kronau and Wocheiner Feistritz (both in the Kreis Radmannsdorf) were subordinated to the Abteilung Zollgrenzschutz Oberkrain in Krainburg; the BZKom (G) Thörl-Maglern (Kreis Villach) was apparently also briefly subordinated to this department.

As to the Abteilung Zollgrenzschutz Kärnten in Lienz, information is also lacking. This department, based in Lienz, was apparently established on the basis of the BefSt des Zollgrenzschutz Lienz (previously HZA Lienz) as part of the IV G office, within the Staatspolizeileitstelle Klagenfurt. Likely subordinated to it were at least the BZKom (G) Hermagor, Mauthen (both in the Kreis Hermagor), and Sillian (in the Kreis Lienz); as far as the *Dienststelle* previously subordinated to the BefSt des Zollgrenzschutzes Villach are concerned, this department took over only the BZKom (G) Thörl-Maglern.

As to the BefSt des Zollgrenzschutzes Villach, its further evolution remains unclear. Surely still active at least until January 1945, the office was later probably gradually dissolved. It is known in fact that in late 1944, an *Abwicklungsstelle*—that is, a special department apparently dedicated exclusively to the dismantling of the office—had been created within the BefSt des Zollgrenzschutzes Villach; this department was still active in late April 1945. In any case, as recalled, it appears certain that between the end of 1944 and the start of 1945, most of its *Dienststelle* still in activity were gradually absorbed into the organizational structures of the Abteilung Zollgrenzschutz Oberkrain in Krainburg and, to a lesser extent, the Abteilung Zollgrenzschutz Kärnten in Lienz.[6]

In regard to the Zollgrenzschutz strength of the units subordinated to the HZA Villach, data are fragmentary and certainly incomplete. According to German sources, in May 1942 this office could rely, within the Kreis Radmannsdorf only, on 236 border guards allocated there, of which thirty-six were officers and two hundred were reservists. On the basis of partisan sources, it seems that, thanks to the setting up and integration of new established posts/outposts in the Oberkrain and OZAK territories, the HZA Villach staff in these areas only later numbered around five hundred men.[7]

3.1
The Main *Dienststelle* of the Hauptzollamt Villach

The organizational structure of the *Dienststelle* subordinated to the HZA Villach is at the moment largely unknown; the following sections are based on the minimal available information. The only organizational chart known related to the HZA Villach's structure dates back to May 1942; however, this document lists only its posts and outposts located in the Oberkrain territory. Two other lists of the *Dienststelle* subordinated to the HZA Villach, certainly incomplete, one of German and one of partisan origin, date to the end of June 1943 and probably to the autumn of 1944, respectively.[8] The backbone of the HZA Villach was certainly formed by the network of the BZKom (G). From the combination of the aforementioned data with information of various origin, it emerges that between 1941 and 1945, subordinated to the HZA Villach had been, for shorter or longer periods, the BZKom (G) Arnoldstein, St. Jakob im Rosental, Obergöriach/Veldes, Kronau, Wocheiner-Feistritz, and, apparently, Thörl-Maglern. The reconstruction of the organizational structures of these commissariats is rather complex.[9]

3.1.1
The Bezirkszollkommissariat (G) Arnoldstein

The BZKom (G) Arnoldstein, also referred to as BZKom (G) Arnoldstein in Riegersdorf-Tschau, was based in Riegersdorf-Tschau (Kreis Villach) and was active from 1939 to the summer of 1943. In May 1941, the headquarters of the BZKom (G) Arnoldstein were transferred for a short period in Kranjska Gora (Kreis Radmannsdorf). Since April 1939, the position of *Bezirkzollkommissar* was held by an officer referred to as BZKom (G) Friedrich Gebhardt, who joined the Reichsfinanzverwaltung in 1920 and had previously occupied the position of BZKom (G) Eisenkappel (HZA Klagenfurt). Gebhardt's adjutant, at least in summer 1942, was apparently Zollinspektor Arno Schott. The BZKom (G) Arnoldstein was dissolved between the end of August and the beginning of September 1943, concurrently with the assignment to Gebhardt of a position at the HZA Villach headquarters. In anticipation of its dissolution, all the still-existing *Dienststelle* subordinated to the BZKom (G) Arnoldstein were gradually disbanded or integrated into the organizational structure of others BZKom (G) (see later). At the end of August 1943, only three posts—it is not known which ones—were in fact subordinated to the BZKom (G) Arnoldstein. During the course of its existence, at least the GASt Arnoldstein, Kronau, Ratschach-Matten, Ratschach-Matten-Süd, the ZASt (G) Kronau, Mallestig, Riegersdorf, and Thörl-Maglern and seemingly also the GASt Feistritz an der Gail were subordinated to the BZKom (G) Arnoldstein.

The GASt Arnoldstein was probably located in Arnoldstein (Kreis Villach). The information about this post is rather scarce; it was apparently subordinated to the BZKom (G) Arnoldstein from August 1939 to June 1943, later being integrated into the organizational structure of the BZKom (G) Kronau. It was also indicated as ZASt (G) Arnoldstein and ZASt (G) (mot.) Arnoldstein or motorized post, the latter being commanded by Zollsekretär Johann Lautner in September 1942.

The GASt Kronau was probably located in Kranjska Gora (Kreis Radmannsdorf). Already active in April 1941, it was subordinated to the BZKom (G) Arnoldstein until April 1942, when it was integrated into the organizational structure of the BZKom (G) Veldes. In 1941–1942 a post indicated as ZASt (G) Kronau was apparently also active in the village, about which no further information is known.

The GASt Ratschach-Matten was based in Rateče-Planica (Kreis Radmannsdorf). It was subordinated to the BZKom (G) Arnoldstein at least from the spring of 1941 to the summer of 1943, later being integrated into the organizational structure of the BZKom (G) Kronau. In May 1942, the position of *Postenführer* of GASt Ratschach-Matten was occupied by Zollassistent Ochsenkuhn. During the same period, the strength of the post amounted to four officers and forty-five reservists. It is likely that it coincided with the post indicated also as ZASt (G) Ratschach-Matten-Nord or simply as ZASt (G) Ratschach-Matten. At least starting from July 1942 the Höhenstützpunkt Strametz-Haus, an altitude outpost located on Mount Ofen (known by Slovenians as Peč and by Italians as Monte Forno; it was the point of conjunction between Kreis Villach, Kreis Radmannsdorf, and Provincia di Udine) was subordinated to the GASt Ratschach-Matten. It seems that the headquarters of the outpost were housed in a structure that no longer exists, adjacent to the current "Planinsko Društvo Peč 1509" hut; the facility was named "Dr. Strametz-Haus" in honor of Regierungsdirektor Andreas Strametz, who held the position of deputy at the Abteilung Zoll within the Oberfinanzpräsidium Graz. Subordinated to the GASt Ratschach-Matten was almost certainly also the Stutzpünkt Richter-Haus, an outpost billeted in the locality of Tamar at the former "Planica" facility of the Graničarji (the Yugoslav border guards); the building, adjacent to the current "Planinski dom Tamar" hut, was renamed "Dr. Richter-Haus" in honor of the Oberfinanzpräsident Graz Richard Richter.

The GASt Ratschach-Matten-Süd, whose exact location remains unknown, was apparently located in the railway station area in the southern part of Rateče-Planica (Kreis Radmannsdorf). Active at least since January 1943, it seems to have had a very short life; it was the same post indicated during 1943 as ZASt (G) Ratschach-Matten-Süd and commanded by Zollsekretär Heinrich Ibler.

The ZASt (G) Mallestig was located in Mallestig (Kreis Villach) and was subordinated to the BZKom (G) Arnoldstein at least from May 1939 to October 1941, later probably being downsized to *Stützpunkt* level. No further information is available on this post.

The ZASt (G) Riegersdorf was probably also located in Riegersdorf-Tschau, but almost nothing is known about it. Active already in May 1939, it was probably disbanded in the autumn of 1941.

The ZASt (G) Thörl-Maglern was probably located in Thörl-Maglern (Kreis Villach) and was active at least since May 1939. In April 1942, the position of *Postenführer* of ZASt (G) Thörl-Maglern seems to have been held by Zollsekretär Michael Moser.

Apparently subordinated to the BZKom (G) Arnoldstein was the GASt Feistritz an der Gail, which was located in Feistritz an der Gail (Kreis Villach) and was already active in 1939 as ZASt (G) Feistritz im Gailtal.

The BZKom (G) Arnoldstein also provided seconded staff for the *Grenzübergangsstelle* of the border crossings of Coccau/Thörl (between Kreis Villach and Provincia di Udine) and Fusine/Rateče (between Kreis Radmannsdorf and Provincia di Udine), on which, however, no detailed information is available.[10]

The town of Arnoldstein (Austria). In the background, on the crest of the Karavanke mountains, the stretch of the Reichsgrenze that ran between the border crossing of Coccau/Thörl and Mount Ofen.

Locality of Dreiländereck / Cippo Tre Confini / Tromeja (junction point between Austria, Italy, and Slovenia), 1944. The BZKom (G) Kronau, Oberzollinspektor Kellerer, posing next to the brand-new border stone C1 (former triborder stone). © *Author's archive*

Locality of Dreiländereck / Cippo Tre Confini / Tromeja (junction point between Austria, Italy, and Slovenia), 1944. The Höhenstützpunkt Strametz-Haus, a facility that no longer exists. © *Kärntner Landesarchiv*

Locality of Dreiländereck / Cippo Tre Confini / Tromeja (junction point between Austria, Italy, and Slovenia), 1950s. Members of the Austrian Zollwache (customs guard) next to the still-standing Höhenstützpunkt Strametz-Haus. © *Wiegele Archive*

Border crossing of Coccau/Thörl (between Italy and Austria), 1930s

Locality of Feistritzer Alm (Feistritz an der Gail, Austria). Border guards of the HZA Villach while patrolling the Reichsgrenze. In this locality was based the Höhenstützpunkt Feistritzer Alm. © *Kärntner Landesarchiv*

Border crossing of Coccau/Thörl (between Italy and Austria), August 1943. SS-Karstwehr-Bataillon units as they cross the border to enter Italy. Note the *Grenzübergangsstelle* and the building of the *Grenzzollstelle*. © *Guido Ronconi*

3.1.2
The Bezirkszollkommissariat (G) St. Jakob im Rosental

The BZKom (G) St. Jakob im Rosental had its headquarters in Maria Elend (Kreis Villach). It was active at least between 1939 and October 1941 and in origin was apparently subordinated to the HZA Klagenfurt. Until June 1941, the position of *Bezirkszollkommissar* was apparently held by an officer referred to as BZKom (G) Anton Frischmann. Subordinated to the BZKom (G) St. Jakob im Rosental were with certainty at least two posts, the ZASt (G) Rosenbach and Woroutz, and apparently also the ZASt (G) Latschach.

The ZASt (G) Rosenbach was probably located in Rosenbach (Kreis Villach) and was active at least between May 1940 and October 1941, probably being disbanded later.

The ZASt (G) Woroutz was probably located in the locality of Woroutz near Unteraichwald (Kreis Villach) and was active at least between May 1939 and October 1941, probably being disbanded later.

The ZASt (G) Latschach was probably based in Latschach (Kreis Villach) and was active at least between October 1939 and April 1941, probably being disbanded later.[11]

3.1.3
The Bezirkszollkommissariat (G) Obergöriach/Veldes

The BZKom (G) Obergöriach apparently had its headquarters in the locality of Rečica, near Bled (Kreis Radmannsdorf), and was already active by the spring of 1941. In August of that year, it seems that the position of BZKom (G) Obergöriach was held by Zollinspektor Bremel. The information on this BZKom (G) is particularly scarce; it seems, however, that already during the course of 1941 the GASt Althammer, Meistern, and Wocheiner-Feistritz were subordinated to it. No detailed information was found on the organizational structure of the aforementioned posts during this specific period of time. Probably at the beginning of 1942, the BZKom (G) Obergöriach changed its name to BZKom (G) Veldes, moving its headquarters to Bled (Kreis Radmannsdorf); later it seems that the headquarters were further moved, for a very short period, to Kranjska Gora (Kreis Radmannsdorf). At least between January 1942 and July 1943, the position of *Bezirkszollkommissar* was held by an officer indicated as BZKom (G) Anton Frischmann, who seems to have been previously BZKom (G) St. Jakob im Rosental; his deputy was apparently Zollinspektor Thoma. In May 1942, the strength of the BZKom (G) Veldes amounted to one BZKom (G), four officers, and five reservists, while the overall staff, including all its subordinated *Dienststelle*, stood at seventeen officers and eighty-nine reservists. The BZKom (G) Veldes was probably dissolved during the summer of 1943; in view of its suppression, all the still-existing posts and outposts subordinated to it seem to have been integrated into the organizational structure of the BZKom (G) Kronau and Wocheiner-Feistritz (see later). During its existence, certainly subordinated to the BZKom (G) Veldes were at least the GASt Althammer, Kronau, Meistern, Mitterdorf in Wochein, and Wocheiner-Feistritz.

The GASt Althammer was probably located in Stara Fužina (Kreis Radmannsdorf). Established within the BZKom (G) Obergöriach as early as the spring of 1941, between March and April 1942 it was apparently integrated into the organizational structure of the BZKom (G) Veldes. During this early time it was also known as GASt Althammer in St. Johann, and therefore it was perhaps initially based, for a brief time, in the nearby settlement of Sv. Janez. Sporadically also indicated as ZASt (G) Althammer, this post was later subordinated to the

BZKom (G) Wocheiner-Feistritz. At least since April 1942, the position of *Postenführer* of ZASt (G) Althammer was occupied by Zollsekretär Heinrich Ziegler. During 1941, subordinated to the BZKom (G) Obergöriach, probably through the GASt Althammer, were two outposts apparently located in the Bohinj basin area and indicated as Stützpunkt Savica (or Savitza) and Höhenstützpunkt Berroth-Hütte. With regard to the Stützpunkt Savica, its exact location is not known; it seems, however, that it could had been located at the Savica sources (Slap Savica) in the locality of "Koča pri Savici," probably by the former Graničarji facility located there. As for the second outpost, during summer 1941 it was referred to as "Stützpunkt Savica dzzt. Höhenstützpunkt Berroth-Hütte"; it is therefore conceivable that at some point the Stützpunkt Savica was moved, perhaps temporarily, at an unknown altitude facility designated as Höhenstützpunkt Berroth-Hütte. This facility was probably renamed in honor of Regierungsrat Dr. Berroth, apparently first director of the Abteilung Zoll of the Oberfinanzpräsidium Graz. In any case, from spring 1942 onward, a Stützpunkt Savitza was again existing in the organizational structure of the newly established BZKom (G) Wocheiner-Feistritz.

The GASt Kronau was based in Kranjska Gora (Kreis Radmannsdorf) at the current Borovška cesta nr. 27, by the former Yugoslav forestry office, in a building renamed "Hoßfeld-Haus" in honor of the Generalinspekteur des Zollgrenzschutzes Johannes Hoßfeld. This post, previously subordinated to the BZKom (G) Arnoldstein, was integrated into the organizational structure of the BZKom (G) Veldes apparently from April 1942 onward. At least since May 1942, the position of *Postenführer* of GASt Kronau was held by Zollsekretär Karl Pfister; during the same period, the post's strength amounted to four officers and thirty-six reservists. Probably in January 1943, the GASt Kronau was integrated into the organizational structure of the newly established BZKom (G) Kronau. In October 1942, an altitude outpost was subordinated to this post; its exact designation is not known but it was apparently referred to as Höhenstützpunkt Mojstrovkapass, also indicated as "Grenzstützpunkt." Its members were billeted at two different structures in the vicinity of the border crossing of Prelaz Vršič (known by the Germans as Mojstrovkapass and by the Italians as Passo della Moistrocca, between Kreis Radmannsdorf and Provincia di Gorizia). The headquarters of the outpost were located around 5 km from the border crossing, at the "Klin" former Graničarji facility now known as "Mihov dom na Vršiču" hut. The building was renamed "Jungk-Haus" in honor of the second director of the Abteilung Zoll of the Oberfinanzpräsidium Graz, Finanzpräsident Jungk, following a total refurbishing by the GASt Kronau staff, on the basis of a project by Pfister himself. According to this project the facility was supposed to be denominated Höhenstützpunkt Jungk-Haus, but there is no confirmation that this name was actually used. The staff assigned to the border crossing was billeted nearby at the current "Erjavčeva koča na Vršiču" hut, a building renamed "Dr. Sperling-Haus" in honor of the Grenzreferent Graz, Regierungsrat Friedrich Sperling. The border guards billeted at the "Dr. Sperling-Haus" manned the border bar at the former "Vršič cesta" sentry box of the Graničarji located next to the Prelaz Vršič border crossing; that structure, not existing anymore, was positioned close to the border stone 6/XV. The border-crossing area, which was almost totally obstructed by a "Grenzsperre" (border blockade) consisting of a thick barrier of barbed wire, was apparently forbidden to nonmilitary traffic. Furthermore, border guards subordinated to the BZKom (G) Veldes were also based in the locality of Krnica, at the current "Dom Krnica" hut, renamed "Dr. Rathke-Haus" in honor of the Vorsteher des HZA Villach, Regierungsrat Rathke, and also indicated as headquarters of the Stützpunkt Rathke-Haus (Krnica-Tal).

The GASt Meistern was located in Mojstrana (Kreis Radmannsdorf) and was sporadically also indicated as ZASt (G) Meistern. Subordinated to the BZKom (G) Obergöriach from April 1941 onward, it was later integrated into the organizational structure of the BZKom (G) Veldes; in summer 1943, it was subordinated to the BZKom (G) Kronau. In May 1942, the position of *Postenführer* of GASt Meistern was occupied by Zollsekretär Stanglmair, previously *Lagerführer* (commander) of the Ausbildungslager des Zollgrenzschutzes Schloss Kreuthberg (see later). During the same period, the strength of the GASt Meistern amounted to five officers and twenty-seven reservists. Subordinated to the GASt Meistern were apparently at least two outposts indicated as Stützpunkt Meistern and Höhenstützpunkt Aljaž-Haus. The information about the Stützpunkt Meistern is very scarce, but it was probably the same outpost indicated in December 1941 as Zollgrenzstützpunkt Mojstrana; its exact location is not known, but during the summer 1943 it was certainly based in the vicinity of Mojstrana, perhaps in the hamlet of Dovje. The Höhenstützpunkt Aljaž-Haus was located in the locality of Vrata, at the current "Aljažev dom v Vratih" hut, later renamed "Kugy-Haus" in honor of the Austro-Hungarian Alpinist Julius Kugy. The position of Stützpunktführer Aljaž-Haus was apparently held by Zollasisstent Wiedergut. Seconded staff of this outpost, perhaps billeted at the former Graničarji facility located on that site, probably monitored the Alpine pass of Luknja (Passo del Forame for the Italians); however, nothing certain is known in this regard. Connected somehow to the Höhenstützpunkt Aljaž-Haus was certainly the Höhenstützpunkt Kredarica-Hütte, an altitude outpost based near the peak of Mount Triglav, at the current "Triglavski dom na Kredarici" hut.

The GASt Mitterdorf in Wochein was located in the village of Srednja vas v Bohinju (Kreis Radmannsdorf). Previously subordinated to the BZKom (G) Obergöriach, it was later integrated into the organizational structure of the BZKom (G) Veldes until the spring of 1943, when it was absorbed into the BZKom (G) Wocheiner-Feistritz. In May 1942, the position of *Postenführer* of GASt Mitterdorf in Wochein was occupied by Zollassistent Johann Walz; during the same period the strength of the post amounted to four officers and twenty-one reservists. In late 1942–early 1943, this post was also indicated as ZASt (G) Mitterdorf in Wochein.

The village of Bled (Slovenia)

The GASt Wocheiner-Feistritz was likely based in Bohinjska Bistrica (Kreis Radmannsdorf). Initially subordinated to the BZKom (G) Obergöriach, it was later integrated into the organizational structure of the BZKom (G) Veldes; as of the spring of 1942 it seems that this post was transferred to the newly established BZKom (G) Wocheiner-Feistritz. The position of *Postenführer* of GASt Wocheiner-Feistritz in January 1942, indicated also as ZASt (G) Wocheiner-Feistritz, was held by Zollassistent Rudolf Eberle.[12]

The "Aljažev dom" hut (Slovenia), 1942–43. The Höhenstützpunkt Aljaž-Haus.
© *Kärntner Landesarchiv*

The "Triglavski dom na Kredarici" hut (Slovenia), 1942–43. Members of the Zollgrenzschutz at the Höhenstützpunkt Kredarica-Hütte. © *Kärntner Landesarchiv and Gorenjski muzej Kranj*

Mount Triglav (Slovenia), 1942–43. Members of the Zollgrenzschutz posing next to the high-altitude storm shelter known as "Aljažev-stolp." © *Kärntner Landesarchiv*

The "Dom Krnica" hut (Kranjska Gora, Slovenia), 1942–43. The "Dr. Rathke-Haus," headquarters of the Stützpunkt Krnica-Tal. © *Kärntner Landesarchiv*

3.1.4
The Bezirkszollkommissariat (G) Kronau

The BZKom (G) Kronau, apparently established since January 1943, was billeted in a building at the current Borovška cesta nr. 27 in Kranjska Gora (Kreis Radmannsdorf). This facility, known as "Hoßfeld-Haus," had previously hosted the headquarters of the GASt Kronau during its subordination to the BZKom (G) Veldes. Regarding the position of BZKom (G) Kronau, the available data are particularly confusing. In early 1943, this office was apparently held by Zollinspektor Dr. Gustav Guanin, who had previously been in service at the HZA Lienz. It seems that in late 1943, Guanin was replaced by the former BZKom (G) Veldes Anton Frischmann. In February 1944, the position of BZKom (G) Kronau was briefly held by an officer referred to as "Zollkommissar" Robert Schmied; during this period the function of his deputy ("Stellvertreter") was held by Guanin. Apparently as of spring 1944, Guanin again took over the position of BZKom (G) Kronau, at least initially as an interim replacement, inasmuch as in September 1944 he referred to himself as "*mit der Leitung beauftragt*" (in charge for the management). During the spring–summer of 1944, it seems that Guanin was momentarily replaced in his functions by the Oberzollinspektor Kellerer, who had previously held the position of BZKom (G) Wocheiner-Feistritz. At least starting from March 1945, the position of *Beamte zur besonderen Verwendung* (Beamte z.b.V., officer with special assistance duties) at the BZKom (G) Kronau was held by Oberzollsekretär Pfister, previously *Postenführer* of GASt Kronau. It is known that the *Stab* of the BZKom (G) Kronau alone numbered around ten border guards. At least from July 1943 and October 1944, respectively, the positions of *Abteilungsführer* in Meistern and *Abteilungsführer* in Thörl-Maglern were created within the BZKom (G) Kronau. These offices, about which very little is known, were led by liaison officers to whom an unspecified number of *Dienststelle* were directly subordinated (see later). As recalled earlier, in late 1944–early 1945, the BZKom (G) Kronau was integrated in the organizational structure of the Abteilung Zollgrenzschutz Oberkrain in Krainburg. In late August 1943, three not-further-specified posts were subordinated to the BZKom (G) Kronau. In any case, during the course of its existence, certainly subordinated to the BZKom (G) Kronau were the GASt Arnoldstein, Feistritz an der Gail, Kronau, Meistern, Ratschach-Matten, Wurzenpass, and, apparently, Thörl-Maglern, as well as the ZASt (G) Kronau.

The central part of the village of Kranjska Gora (Slovenia). In the background, Mounts Prisojnik and Razor, part of the Julian Alps range, along whose crests ran the Reichsgrenze.

Kranjska Gora (Slovenia), the current Borovška cesta nr. 27, as seen in 1944. The main entrance of the "Hoßfeld-Haus" during its occupation by the BZKom (G) Kronau. © *Kärntner Landesarchiv*

Kranjska Gora (Slovenia), the current Borovška cesta nr. 27, 1941–42. The main entrance of the "Hoßfeld-Haus" during the stay of the GASt Kronau. © *Kärntner Landesarchiv*

Kranjska Gora (Slovenia), the current
Borovška cesta nr. 27. Decorations inside
the "Hoßfeld-Haus."
© *Kärntner Landesarchiv*

Kranjska Gora (Slovenia), the current Borovška cesta nr. 27. The "Hoßfeld-Haus" building. © *Kärntner Landesarchiv*

Kranjska Gora (Slovenia), the current Borovška cesta nr. 7, March 1944. The headquarters of the ZASt (G) Kronau. © *Author's archive and Kärntner Landesarchiv*

The GASt Arnoldstein, as mentioned, was probably based in Arnoldstein (Kreis Villach). This post, previously subordinated to the BZKom (G) Arnoldstein, starting at least from autumn 1943 was integrated into the structure of the BZKom (G) Kronau, probably being disbanded in the summer of 1944.

The GASt Feistritz an der Gail was probably based in Feistriz an der Gail (Kreis Villach). This post also seems to have been previously subordinated to the BZKom (G) Arnoldstein, being later, probably as early as spring–summer 1943, integrated into the organizational structure of the BZKom (G) Kronau. During autumn 1944, the GASt Feistritz an der Gail was subordinated to the BZKom (G) Kronau, probably through the *Abteilungsführer* in Thörl-Maglern, while in December of the same year it was subordinated to the newly established BZKom (G) Thörl-Maglern.

The GASt Kronau was based in Kranjska Gora (Kreis Radmannsdorf); however, it is not clear whether it was still stationed at the "Hoßfeld-Haus." This post, previously subordinated to the BZKom (G) Veldes, was integrated into the structure of the BZKom (G) Kronau starting in the summer of 1943. To the GASt Kronau was still subordinated the Höhenstützpunkt Mojstrovkapass, whose members, as mentioned, were billeted at the "Jungk-Haus" and at the "Dr. Sperling-Haus" at the pass of Prelaz Vršič (between Kreis Radmannsdorf and Provincia di Gorizia) and provided the personnel for the monitoring and the security of the border crossing located there. At least during 1944, the position of *Stützpunktführer* at Mojstrovkapass was held by Zollassistent Doujak. As a consequence of the Italian armistice of September 8, 1943, perhaps in anticipation of a possible resurgence of partisan activity in the Provincia di Gorizia, the Höhenstützpunkt Mojstrovkapass was reinforced. Members of the Zollgrenzschutz, certainly subordinated to the outpost, were in fact billeted at the former summer detachment "Moistrocca" of the Guardia di Finanza (the Italian Finance Guard), located on the Italian side of the border and nowadays known as "Tičarjev dom" hut. Furthermore, at least since the end of September 1943, a border outpost was apparently activated at the secondary border crossing a few tens of meters away from the "Tičarjev dom." The border guards assigned to the control of this secondary path, also billeted at the "Dr. Sperling-Haus," apparently served at the former "Vršič vrh" facility of the Graničarji (the current "Poštarski dom na Vršiču" hut) and at the near bunker, still existing, located on the Italian side of the border, close to the border stone 7/XI. During the spring of 1944 was also active a ZASt (G) Kronau, a post that already existed at least from 1941–1942. At the present day it remains unclear if this post actually replaced the GASt Kronau in all its functions or if the latter was just renamed ZASt (G) Kronau. In any case, the ZASt (G) Kronau was located, at least from March 1944 until the end of the war, at the current Borovška cesta nr. 7 in Kranjska Gora; it was also indicated as ZASt (G) (mot.) or motorized post. In February 1944, the position of *Postenführer* of ZASt (G) Kronau was held by Zollsekretär Thomas Helmer, replaced during the same year by an officer indicated, by partisan sources, as "Zollkommissar" Winkler. In early 1944, the ZASt (G) Kronau numbered around thirty border guards. Apparently subordinated to the ZASt (G) Kronau was the Talstützpunkt Wurzen, an outpost located in the village of Podkoren (Kreis Radmannsdorf), also referred to as "Zollgrenzschutz-Stützpunkt" and manned by seven border guards; in February 1944, the position of *Stützpunktführer* at Wurzen was held by Zollsekretär Franz Erber, later replaced by Zollassistent Paik (or Palk). According to some unclear information, the Stützpunkt Wald, an outpost billeted at the Gauschule (training school for officers of the NSDAP) based at the Hotel "Coop" in Gozd Martuljek (Kreis

Radmannsdorf), apparently was also subordinated to the ZASt (G) Kronau. In 1944, the command of these border guards was entrusted to Zollassistent Brugger. During wintertime the Hotel "Coop" apparently also hosted the personnel of the various Höhenstützpunkt subordinated to the BZKom (G) Kronau, which became uninhabitable due to heavy snow.

"Mihov dom" hut (Slovenia), 1942. The Zollgrenzschutz watch at the former "Klin" facility of the Graničarji, base of the Höhenstützpunkt Mojstrovkapass.
© *Kärntner Landesarchiv*

"Mihov dom" hut (Slovenia), 1943. The renovations to the "Klin" facility. Note the personal vehicle of the BZKom (G) Kronau, Zollinspektor Guanin, a Tempo G 1200 with license plate K-25014 (Kärnten) and the "ZOLL" sign. It was probably the chassis number 1263898, acquired by the Oberfinanzpräsidium Graz in July 1942. © *Kärntner Landesarchiv*

"Mihov dom" hut (Slovenia), 1943. The "Klin" facility, renovated by the Zollgrenzschutz and renamed "Jungk-Haus." © *Kärntner Landesarchiv*

"Mihov dom" hut (Slovenia), 1943–44. Zollsekretär Pfister at the entrance of the "Jungk-Haus." © *Kärntner Landesarchiv*

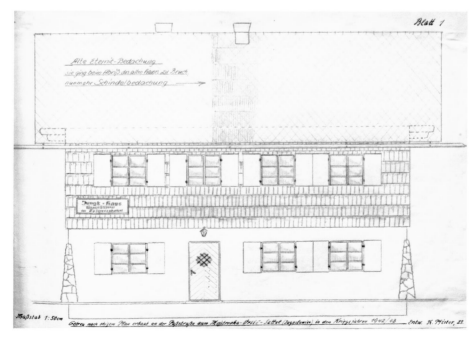

The renovation project of the former "Klin" facility of the Graničarji drawn by Zollsekretär Pfister. © *Kärntner Landesarchiv*

"Erjavčeva koča na Vršiču" hut (Slovenia), 1943–44. The "Dr. Sperling-Haus," detached headquarters of the Höhenstützpunkt Mojstrovkapass. © *Kärntner Landesarchiv*

"Erjavčeva koča na Vršiču" hut (Slovenia), 1943–44. The *Stützpunktfüher* at Mojstrovkapass, Zollassistent Doujak, *on the right*, cleans a Breda Mod. 30 war booty Italian machine gun outside the "Dr. Sperling-Haus." © *Kärntner Landesarchiv*

"Koča na Gozdu pod Vršičem" hut (Slovenia) 1943. The Tempo G 1200, personal vehicle of BZKom (G) Kronau, Zollinspektor Guanin (*first on the right*), with the "ZOLL" sign. On the left is Zollsekretär Pfister. © *Kärntner Landesarchiv*

Prelaz Vršič (Slovenia), 1943–44. Border guards of the Höhenstützpunkt Mojstrovkapass with a *Zollhund* serving at the "Vršič cesta" former Graničarji sentry box; it was located at the border crossing near the boundary stone 6/XV. © *Kärntner Landesarchiv*

Prelaz Vršič (Slovenia), 1944. "Peter der Kleine," the mule of the BZKom (G) Kronau, crossing the Reichsgrenze in order to transport supplies to the border guards billeted on the Italian side of the border. © *Kärntner Landesarchiv*

Prelaz Vršič (Slovenia), 1944. The BZKom (G) Kronau, Zollinspektor Guanin (*in the middle*), chatting with the *Stützpunktführer* at Mojstrovkapass, Zollassistent Doujak (*on the right*). © *Kärntner Landesarchiv*

"Poštarski dom na Vršiču" hut (Prelaz Vršič, Slovenia), 1943–44. After September 1943, border guards of the Höhenstützpunkt Mojstrovkapass were also in service at this hut. © *Kärntner Landesarchiv*

Prelaz Vršič (Slovenia), 1943–44. Members of the Zollgrenzschutz at the bunker, now gone, located on the Italian side of the border crossing, in the clearing of the current pass souvenir shop. Note the barbed-wire blockade known as "Grenzsperre Mojstrovkapass" and the *Zollhund*. © *Kärntner Landesarchiv*

Locality of "Poštarski dom na Vršiču" (Prelaz Vršič, Slovenia), 1943–44. Members of the Zollgrenzschutz near the bunker, still existing, located on the Italian side of the border near the Alpine hut. © *Kärntner Landesarchiv*

"Tičarjev dom" hut (Prelaz Vršič, Slovenia), 1942–43. Members of the Zollgrenzschutz and of the Guardia di Finanza portrayed in front of the entrance of the "Moistrocca" summer detachment, before the Italian armistice. © *Kärntner Landesarchiv*

"Tičarjev dom" hut (Prelaz Vršič, Slovenia), 1943–44. Members of the Zollgrenzschutz, billeted at the "Moistrocca" summer detachment of the Guardia di Finanza, after the Italian armistice. © *Kärntner Landesarchiv*

"Tičarjev dom" hut (Prelaz Vršič, Slovenia), 1943–44. The Vorsteher des HZA Villach, Zollrat Rapf (wearing a tunic made of Italian M29 camo fabric) chatting with the *Stützpunktführer* at Mojstrovkapass, Zollassistent Doujak. © *Kärntner Landesarchiv*

Locality of Velika Planina (Prelaz Vršič, Slovenia), 1943–44. The *Stützpunktführer* at Mojstrovkapass, Zollassistent Doujak, in front of the entrance of the Italian fort "nr. 2," located on the slopes of the "Grebenec." © *Kärntner Landesarchiv*

Prelaz Vršič (Slovenia), 1943–44. Zollsekretär Pfister posing near the "Cheval de Frise" at an unknown location, possibly in the area of the "Poštarski dom na Vršiču." Note the unidentified facility in the background. © *Kärntner Landesarchiv*

The GASt Meistern was located in Mojstrana (Kreis Radmannsdorf). Initially subordinated to the BZKom (G) Veldes, from the summer of 1943 this post was integrated into the organizational structure of the BZKom (G) Kronau. During 1944, the position of *Postenführer* of GASt Meistern was held by Zollsekretär Peter Bauer. Furthermore, at least starting from July 1943, the position of *Abteilungsführer* in Meistern was created within the BZKom (G) Kronau, which in February 1944 was held by Bauer himself. In this function of liaison officer he had twenty border guards and an unspecified number of *Dienststelle* directly subordinated to him; they likely included at least the GASt Meistern, the Einsatzgruppe Meistern, the Übungslager für Zollhunde (the customs-duty dog-training camp of Mojstrana; see later), and the Höhenstützpunkt Aljaž-Haus, based in the locality of Vrata (Kreis Radmannsdorf).

The GASt Ratschach-Matten was located in Rateče-Planica (Kreis Radmannsdorf). This post, previously subordinated to the BZKom (G) Arnoldstein, starting from summer 1943 was integrated into the structure of the BZKom (G) Kronau, likely remaining active until the end of the war. In February 1944, the position of *Postenführer* of GASt Ratschach-Matten was held by Zollsekretär Heinrich Ibler, previously *Postenführer* of ZASt (G) Ratschach-Matten-Süd, who was replaced in his functions, during the same year, by Zollsekretär Meier. It seems certain that in this period at least two outposts were subordinated to the GASt Ratschach-Matten: the aforementioned Höhenstützpunkt Strametz-Haus and Stutzpünkt Richter-Haus. The information about them is very scarce; however, it is known that in the autumn of 1944, the position of *Stützpunktführer* at Strametz-Haus was held by an officer indicated by partisan sources as "Zollkommissar" Hagn; he is probably identifiable with Hilfszollassistent Hagn, already in service in Rateče-Planica since July 1942.

Locality of Tamar (Rateče-Planica, Slovenia), 1944. The building on the right was the base of the Stützpunkt Richter-Haus. © *Kärntner Landesarchiv*

Locality of Tamar (Rateče-Planica, Slovenia), 1944. Zollsekretär Pfister (*on the left*) and Oberzollinspektor Kellerer (*in the middle*) posing next to the Stützpunkt Richter-Haus in front of the massif of the Jalovec. © *Author's archive and Kärntner Landesarchiv*

Locality of Tamar (Rateče-Planica, Slovenia), early 1940s. Members of the Zollgrenzschutz in front of the Stützpunkt Richter-Haus. © *Wiegele Archive*

Rateče-Planica (Slovenia), 1941–42. One of the Zollgrenzschutz facilities apparently located in the village, perhaps the headquarters of the GASt Ratschach-Matten-Süd. It has not been possible to identify the exact location of this building, but maybe it originally belonged to the complex of the former railway station (current area of house nr. 161 in Rateče). © *Košir Archive*

Border crossing of Fusine/Rateče (between Italy and Slovenia), 1941–42. The border stone 2/XII near the passage, seen from the German side (note the "D" letter carved on the stone, which stood for "Deutschland"). © *Košir Archive*

Border crossing of Fusine/Rateče (between Italy and Slovenia), 1943–44. Two members of Zollgrenzschutz, with their sidecar with license plate K-400021 (Kärnten), chatting with a man of the Guardia di Finanza; note the obsolete green arm band with the oval plaque of the Zollgrenzschutz auxiliaries worn by the "Finanziere," who was probably subordinated to the BZKom (G) Kronau. © *Kärntner Landesarchiv*

Fusine-Laghi (Italy), 1943–44. The Zollgrenzschutz sidecar with license plate K-400021 (Kärnten) pictured in front of Mount Mangart. © *Author's archive*

Fusine-Laghi (Italy), 1943–44. Border guards subordinated to the BZKom (G) Kronau pose near a huge "Fascio Littorio" at an unidentified facility; it was almost certainly the flagpole of some barracks of the Guardia alla Frontiera (Italian border defense troops) located close to the Reichsgrenze in the "Monte Cavallar-Monte Forno" sector. © *Kärntner Landesarchiv*

Fusine-Laghi (Italy), 1944. Zollsekretär Pfister, driving the BMW sidecar with license plate St-8220 (Steiermark), and Oberzollinspektor Kellerer at one of the Guardia alla Frontiera barracks located close to the Reichsgrenze in the "Monte Cavallar-Monte Forno" sector. © *Author's archive and Kärntner Landesarchiv*

The GASt Wurzenpass was located at the Wurzenpass/Korensko sedlo (Alpine pass between Kreis Villach and Kreis Radmannsdorf), along the "*Polizeigrenze*" line. In January 1945, the position of *Postenführer* of GASt Wurzenpass was apparently held by Hilfszollassistent Hylarius Paterno. Some sources referred to this post also as *Stützpunkt*, so its actual organizational structure remains unclear. It is also known that a Straßenzollamt Wurzenpass was already active in 1939; it is not, however, clear whether there was a connection between the two *Dienststelle*.

Podkoren (Slovenia). The headquarters of the Talstützpunkt Wurzen, apparently located in the meadows surrounding the village church. © *Kärntner Landesarchiv*

The Wurzenpass (between Austria and Slovenia), late 1930s. © *Wiegele Archive*

The Wurzenpass (between Austria and Slovenia) after the war, during the British occupation of Carinthia

Road Podkoren-Wurzenpass (Slovenia), 1944. Service car of the Zollgrenzschutz with license plate St-2783 (Steiermark) parked near the current "Kranjska Gora Parking"; *on the left*, Zollsekretär Pfister; *in the middle*, Oberzollinspektor Kellerer. © *Author's archive*

The GASt Thörl-Maglern was based in Thörl-Maglern (Kreis Villach). From the late summer of 1943, this post was integrated into the organizational structure of the BZKom (G) Kronau; it was most likely the same one previously known as ZASt (G) Thörl-Maglern, which was subordinated to the BZKom (G) Arnoldstein. At least in September 1944, the position of *Postenführer* of GASt Thörl-Maglern was held by Zollsekretär Heinrich Ibler, previously *Postenführer* of GASt Ratschach-Matten, who was killed in action on November 14, 1944 (see later). During the autumn of 1944, the GASt Thörl-Maglern was subordinated to the BZKom (G) Kronau through the *Abteilungsführer* in Thörl-Maglern.

Along with the GASt Feistritz an der Gail and Thörl-Maglern, probably subordinated to the *Abteilungsführer* in Thörl-Maglern were some other *Dienststelle*, among which were the outposts and the warehouses of the Ausweichlager des Zollgrenzschutzes Villach in Töbring and the Stützpunkt Mallestig, all of which were based in the Kreis Villach (see later).

Furthermore, according to a partisan report, it seems that at least from mid-December 1944, the BZKom (G) Kronau had set up an outpost in Italian territory, in Fusine in Valromana (Provincia di Udine), manned by around forty border guards. No additional data were found in this regard.

The BZKom (G) Kronau also provided seconded staff for the *Grenzübergangsstelle* of the border crossings of Coccau/Thörl (between Kreis Villach and Provincia di Udine) and Fusine/Rateče (between Kreis Radmannsdorf and Provincia di Udine).

Following the Italian armistice of September 8, 1943, border guards of the BZKom (G) Kronau were widely employed in the reconnaissance and registration of the fortified works of the "Vallo Alpino del Littorio," located on Italian territory, along the Grenzabschnitt subordinated to it.[13]

3.1.5
The Bezirkszollkommissariat (G) Wocheiner-Feistritz

The BZKom (G) Wocheiner-Feistritz, established at least since the spring of 1942, was based at house nr. 143 in Bohinjska Bistrica (Kreis Radmannsdorf), at the former Yugoslav railway customs office; the building, acquired by the Reichsfinanzverwaltung, was located in the railway station complex. At least until the autumn of 1943, the position of BZKom (G) Wocheiner-Feistritz was held by Zollinspektor Kellerer. During the spring of 1944, this position was apparently held by an officer indicated as BZKom (G) Schmid, who was in turn replaced, during the summer, by the BZKom (G) Walter Kasischke, who had previously been BZKom (G) Drachenburg (HZA Cilli). At the end of March 1945, Kasischke was temporarily replaced by Kriminalsekretär Hugo Schierghofer, a Gestapo officer from Abt. V of the KdS Veldes. Deputy of the BZKom (G) Wocheiner-Feistritz was, at least in late 1943, Zollsekretär Treml; in spring 1944, Zollsekretär Inzenhofer; and in 1945, Zollinspektor Herppich. Secretary of the BZKom (G) Wocheiner-Feistritz was Zollsekretär, later Oberzollsekretär, Gröschel, already Beamte z.b.V. within the same office; in the spring of 1945, the position of Beamte z.b.V. at the BZKom (G) Wocheiner-Feistritz was apparently held by Hilfszollassistent Karl Budde. As recalled earlier, in late 1944–early 1945, the BZKom (G) Wocheiner-Feistritz was integrated in the organizational structure of the Abteilung Zollgrenzschutz Oberkrain in Krainburg. In May 1942, the strength of the *Stab* of the BZKom (G) Wocheiner-Feistritz alone stood at one BZKom (G), three officers, and three reservists, while in February 1944 it amounted to fifteen border guards. As of May 1942, its total staff, including all the *Dienststelle* subordinated to it, stood at thirteen officers and sixty-six reservists. Subsequently, the staff available to the BZKom (G) Wocheiner-Feistritz increased substantially: during December 1944, it additionally acquired nine officers and 210 reservists, while in March 1945 its staff amounted to eleven officers and 205 reservists, including sixteen local Hilfswilliger (local volunteers). The BZKom (G) Wocheiner-Feistritz organizational structure is particularly complex, and it remains partially unclear. In August 1943, the BZKom (G) Wocheiner-Feistritz could count exclusively on four posts, among which certainly those indicated as GASt Wocheiner-Feistritz and Wocheinersee. However, during its existence, at least the GASt Althammer, Mitterdorf in Wochein, St. Johann am Wocheinersee, Wocheiner-Feistritz, Wocheiner-Feistritz-Nord, Wocheiner-Feistritz-West, Wocheiner-Feistritz-Süd, and Wocheinersee were subordinated to it.

The GASt Althammer, initially also referred to as GASt Althammer in St. Johann, was in this period located at house nr. 14 in Stara Fužina (Kreis Radmannsdorf). Previously subordinated to the BZKom (G) Veldes, at least from May 1942 it was integrated into the organizational structure of the BZKom (G) Wocheiner-Feistritz. During the same period the position of *Postenführer* of GASt Althammer was held by Zollsekretär Heinrich Ziegler, and the strength of the post amounted to six officers and thirty-five reservists. Between September 1943 and May 1944, Hilfszollsekretär Josef Spörk held the position of *Postenführer i.V.* (deputy commander of the post). At least from the spring of 1942, subordinated to the GASt Althammer was the Stützpunkt Savica (or Savitza), an outpost whose exact location remains unknown; it seems that it was based near the Savica springs (locally known as Slap Savica), in the locality of "Koča pri Savici," possibly at the former Graničarji facility located there. In this period the position of *Stützpunktführer* at Savitza was occupied by Zollassistent Schwebel. Subordinated to the GASt Althammer was also an altitude outpost, whose exact designation is not known but was apparently referred to as Höhenstützpunkt Bogatin-Sattel, whose staff monitored the high-altitude pass and border crossing of Bogatinsko sedlo (known by the Italians as Passo Bogatin, between Kreis Radmannsdorf, and Provincia di Gorizia); the outpost was certainly operational during 1943 but had probably already been activated during the previous years. It is not clear where the staff of the Höhenstützpunkt Bogatin-Sattel was billeted; according to insufficiently detailed information, it seems that unspecified Zollgrenzschutz personnel were initially stationed at the current "Dom na Komni" hut, a structure known to the Germans as "Komna-Haus" that was set on fire by the partisans in the summer of 1943. Later it seems that the border guards were moved to the "Kärntner-Haus," hypothetically identified with the current "Koča pod Bogatinom" hut. The GASt Althammer was probably dissolved in the spring of 1944; following its suppression, the Stützpunkt Savica and the Höhenstützpunkt Bogatin-Sattel were apparently integrated into the organizational structure of the GASt St. Johann am Wocheinersee.

The GASt Mitterdorf in Wochein was located in Srednja vas v Bohinju (Kreis Radmannsdorf). Previously subordinated to the BZKom (G) Veldes, at least from May 1943 it was integrated into the structure of the BZKom (G) Wocheiner-Feistritz. It is possible that during this transfer of responsibilities, this post was temporarily downsized to *Stützpunkt* level; at the end of May 1943, in fact, Hilfszollsekretär Josef Spörk was referred to as "Stützpunktführer Mitterdorf in Wochein." Spörk was killed in action on May 23, 1944 (see later). In any case, in July 1943 the post was indicated also as ZASt (G) Mitterdorf in Wochein. No further information was found regarding this post; however, it is possible that it was dissolved in the spring of 1944, and that its staff was later integrated into other posts, including the GASt Wocheiner-Feistritz-Nord.

The GASt St. Johann am Wocheinersee, also rarely indicated as ZASt (G) St. Johann am Wocheinersee, was apparently based at the house nr. 39 in Sv. Janez (Kreis Radmannsdorf), hypothetically at the Hotel "Sv. Janez." Active at least from the spring of 1942 until the summer of 1944, it seems that it coincided with the post known as GASt Wocheinersee; however, the information in this regard remains very confusing. Some insufficiently detailed sources indicate, as subordinated to the GASt St. Johann am Wocheinersee, an unidentified Zollgrenzschutz outpost located near the settlement of Ukanc; it could actually have been the aforementioned Stützpunkt Savica of the GASt Althammer, apparently based in the locality of "Koča pri Savici" and later integrated into the organizational structure of the GASt St. Johann am Wocheinersee. Following the dissolution of the GASt Althammer, it is likely that the aforementioned Höhenstützpunkt Bogatin-Sattel was also subordinated to the GASt St. Johann am Wocheinersee. By order of the HSSPF im Wehrkreis XVIII, following the ransacking of the villa of SS-Obergruppenführer Gottlob Berger (head of the SS-Hauptamt in Berlin) located in Sv. Janez, which occurred in May 1943, during which an *SS-Oberscharführer* guarding the building went missing, members of the GASt St. Johann am Wocheinersee were used for securing the property.

The GASt Wocheiner-Feistritz was based at house nr. 177 in Bohinjska Bistrica (Kreis Radmannsdorf), at the "Finančna kontrola" former Graničarji main barracks ("ehem. Graničarjkaserne Stabsgebäude"), a building taken over by the Reichsfinanzverwaltung following the creation of the Oberkrain. Active between spring 1942 and spring 1945, in summer 1943 it was also referred to as GASt (mot.) Wocheiner-Feistritz, or motorized post; it was also known as ZASt (G) Wocheiner-Feistritz. In May 1942, the chair of the *Postenführer* of GASt

Wocheiner-Feistritz was still held by Zollassistent Rudolf Eberle, who was replaced in his functions, at least starting from March 1945, by Zollsekretär Erich Bartheloff. In February 1945, the position of "*stellv. Postenführer*" (deputy commander of the post) was occupied by Zollsekretär Eugen Pfluger, an officer seconded to the BZKom (G) Wocheiner-Feistritz from the GASt Sairach (HZA Krainburg). In May 1942, the strength of the post amounted to four officers and twenty-eight reservists, while in February 1944 it numbered thirty border guards. It is conceivable that in December 1944, a substantial number of border guards belonging to the recently dissolved GASt Wocheiner-Feistritz-Süd were integrated into this post.

The GASt Wocheiner-Feistritz-Nord, whose exact location remains unknown, was perhaps set up in place of the GASt Mitterdorf in Wochein, which at that time was in the process of being dissolved. Apparently active from the first quarter of 1944, the GASt Wocheiner-Feistritz-Nord was probably dissolved before the end of the same year. It likely coincided with the post indicated in March 1944 as ZASt (G) Wocheiner-Feistritz-Nord.

The GASt Wocheiner-Feistritz-West was located at house nr. 88 in Bohinjska Bistrica (Kreis Radmannsdorf). It was active at least during the course of 1944, until the spring of 1945. During 1944, the position of *Postenführer* of GASt Wocheiner-Feistritz-West was held by Zollsekretär Karl Oberhaus, who was replaced at least as of March 1945 by Zollsekretär Broszeit, previously in service at the GASt Schwarzenberg-Ost (HZA Krainburg).

The GASt Wocheiner-Feistritz-Süd was also located, according to partisan sources, at the former Graničarji barracks of Bohinjska Bistrica, which in this case is perhaps to be understood as the customs facility located in the locality of Rovti, near the current "Mencingerjeva Koča" hut (Kreis Radmannsdorf). It was active throughout the course of 1944. The position of *Postenführer* of GASt Wocheiner-Feistritz-Süd was held by Zollsekretär Max Exner, who apparently had previously been commander of the Jagdkommando des Zollgrenzschutzes Meistern and was killed in action on November 14, 1944 (see later). It seems that the GASt Wocheiner-Feistritz-Süd was dissolved following the death of Exner and that the border guards belonging to the post were subsequently integrated into the GASt Wocheiner-Feistritz.

The GASt Wocheinersee, whose exact location remains unknown, was active at least from the spring of 1942 to December 1944. Also sporadically referred to, in late 1943, as ZASt (G) Wocheinersee, it would seem conceivable that it coincided with the post indicated as GASt St. Johann am Wocheinersee. However, on the basis of the scarce, unclear, and at times contradictory data, at the moment this hypothesis cannot be verified. In February 1944, the position of *Postenführer* of GASt Wocheinersee was held by Zollsekretär Johann Lautner, previously *Postenführer* of GASt Arnoldstein.

Subordinated to the BZKom (G) Wocheiner-Feistritz were also some posts located outside the Kreis Radmannsdorf, such as the GASt Dautscha, Petersberg, Piedicolle, and Zarz. Probably due to their isolated positions, located in rural areas of the Kreis Krainburg and of the Provincia di Gorizia subjected to intense partisan activity, it seems that these posts had been subordinated to the BZKom (G) Wocheiner-Feistritz through Zollinspektor Karl Herppich. In fact, starting from autumn 1944, Herppich held the position of *Abteilungsführer* in Petersberg and, as liaison officer, at least a "*vorgeschobener Posten in ital. Gebiet*" (outpost on Italian territory) was subordinated to him, identifiable with the GASt Piedicolle and two posts located in an area indicated as subject to partisan control between the village of Novaki (Provincia di Gorizia) and the Jelovica plateau (between the Kreis Krainburg and Kreis Radmannsdorf), likely to be identified with the GASt Dautscha and GASt Zarz. Therefore, as mentioned earlier, in this way the jurisdiction of the HZA Villach / BefSt des Zollgrenzschutzes Villach was extended also over territories belonging to the Kreis Krainburg and the Provincia di Gorizia. On the basis of unclear data, it appears likely but unconfirmed that the position of *Abteilungsführer* in Petersberg had been activated as early as December 1943 and entrusted to Zollinspektor Rudolf Schaffer. The reconstruction of the organizational structure of the *Abteilungsführer* in Petersberg is particularly complex.

The GASt Dautscha was located in the scattered settlement known as the Davča (Kreis Krainburg), but its exact location remains unknown. The information related to this *Dienststelle* is very confusing. Active already in May 1942 as Stützpunkt Dautscha, it was subordinated, through the GASt Zarz, to the BZKom (G) Laak-West (HZA Krainburg); in this period the strength of the outpost amounted to one officer and forty reservists. Between October 1942 and October 1943, the stronghold was indicated as Zollstützpunkt, ZASt (G), ZGASt (?), GASt Dautscha, and also GASt Eisnern in Dautscha, whose meaning remains unclear. Probably starting from the second half of October 1943, the post was integrated into the organizational structure of the BZKom (G) Wocheiner-Feistritz. In December 1943, when it was officially renamed GASt Dautscha, it seems that it was located in the hamlet of Davča, and the position of *Postenführer* was apparently held by Zollsekretär Brunner. In the same period, subordinated to the GASt Dautscha was the Stützpunkt Zollstrasse, probably located on the German side of the border crossing of Petrovo Brdo (known by Italians as Passo di Colle Pietro and locally indicated also as "Pachmann" crossing, between Kreis Krainburg and Provincia di Gorizia), at the former Graničarji facility (the still-existing sentry box at house nr. 2 in the locality of Podporezen). It was in all likelihood the same outpost apparently subordinated, in March 1943, to the GASt Zarz (HZA Krainburg) and indicated as Stützpunkt Zarz-Zollstrasse (see later). In March 1944, a GASt Dautscha a/Petersberg was also active, about which it has not been possible to find further information; it apparently arose from the merger of the GASt Dautscha with the GASt Petersberg, based in Petrovo Brdo (Provincia di Gorizia). During the same period the position of *Postenführer* of GASt Dautscha a/Petersberg was held by Zollassistent Otto Guth, who had previously been indicated as "GASt-Führer Zarz."

The GASt Petersberg was located at house nr. 1 in Petrovo Brdo (Provincia di Gorizia), at the former "sottotenente Ennio Poggiolini" barracks of the Guardia di Finanza. This post was apparently formed by the BZKom (G) Wocheiner-Feistritz during late 1943. Its organizational structure is not clear enough, since it was sometimes indicated also as Stützpunkt Petersberg. In late 1944, the position of *Postenführer* of GASt Petersberg was occupied by Zollsekretär Georg Stelzer, who would apparently go missing in action as of March 1945, perhaps as a consequence of his transfer for a specialization course at the Ausbildungslager des Zollgrenzschutzes Schloss Neustein (see later). From mid-March 1945, Stelzer was replaced by Zollsekretär Braun, who was referred to as "*GASt-Führer*." It seems that at some point the GASt Petersberg incorporated the GASt Dautscha, creating the GASt Dautscha a/Petersberg, but this is unconfirmed. In any case, the Zollgrenzschutz post of Petrovo Brdo, whose strength, according to partisan sources, was around seventy-five border guards, remained active at least until mid-April 1945.

The GASt Piedicolle was probably located in Podbrdo (Provincia di Gorizia). Border guards subordinated to the BZKom (G) Wocheiner-Feistritz were apparently located in that village as early as mid-October 1943; however, also in this case, the information is not sufficiently clear. The headquarters of the GASt Piedicolle was also indicated as "Zarz/Piedicolle";

the meaning of this designation is not clear, but it is conceivable that at some point this post was downsized to *Stützpunkt* level and subordinated to the GASt Zarz. In any case, it is known that in January 1944, the tasks of this post were referred to as *Zollaufsichtsdienst* (customs inspection), possibly related to the railway traffic of the Wocheiner-Tunnel (Bohinjski predor, the railway tunnel Bohinjska Bistrica–Podbrdo, which connected the Kreis Radmannsdorf with the Provincia di Gorizia); for this reason it is most likely that the post was considered a "vorgeschobene Zollstelle," which was a customs office based close to the Reichsgrenze but on foreign territory. On April 28, 1945, when the Baška Grapa valley (Provincia di Gorizia) had already been, at least in part, occupied by partisan forces, this *Dienststelle* was referred to as Stützpunkt Piedicolle; formed by two groups of border guards, it was mainly used for securing the southern entrance of the Wocheiner-Tunnel and the Petrovo Brdo–Sorica road, considered important for communication to the Reich.

The GASt Zarz, sporadically referred to as ZASt (G) Zarz, was based in Sorica (Kreis Krainburg) at house nr. 1 ("Pfarrhof Ober-Zarz" or parish of Zgornja Sorica) and nr. 2 ("Schulegebäude Unter-Zarz" or schools of Spodnja Sorica). Again the sources related to its structure are not sufficiently clear. Apparently active since spring 1941, the post was initially subordinated to the BZKom (G) Laak-West (HZA Krainburg). On the basis of German sources, it is known that in May 1942 the strength of GASt Zarz amounted to six officers and forty-one reservists. Probably due to its isolated position, located within a particularly impervious area and subject to intense partisan activity, perhaps to facilitate territorial control, at least starting from mid-October 1943 this post was subordinated to the BZKom (G) Wocheiner-Feistritz, being effectively integrated into the structure of the HZA Villach. It appears that the position of *Postenführer* of GASt Zarz was initially held by Zollsekretär Josef Heim and later by Zollsekretär Erich Schomaker, who was killed by partisans on May 24, 1943. In December 1943, it was certainly occupied by Zollassistent Otto Guth, who was previously at the ZASt (G) Druschtsche (HZA Cilli); Guth, also referred to as "*GASt-Führer*," was replaced in his functions, at least from the second semester of 1944, by Zollsekretär Georg Kellner, who apparently came from the ZASt (G) Druschtsche as well. During 1943, it was subordinated to the GASt Zarz an outpost known as Stützpunkt Zarz-Zollstrasse, probably located on the German side of the border crossing of Petrovo Brdo (between Kreis Krainburg and Provincia di Gorizia), at the former Graničarji facility (the still-existing sentry box at house nr. 2 in the locality of Podporezen); it was apparently also indicated as Stützpunkt Zarz-Landstrasse, so its official designation remains unclear. This outpost seems to have been later integrated into the GASt Dautscha organizational structure as Stützpunkt Zollstrasse. The GASt Zarz remained certainly active until April 1945. According to partisan sources, the post reached a maximum staff of about ninety border guards, including some local Hilfswilliger.

Also part of the organizational structure of the BZKom (G) Wocheiner-Feistritz was another altitude outpost, located in the Bohinj basin area (Kreis Radmannsdorf), whose direct subordination remains unknown. Indicated in autumn 1942 as Höhenstützpunkt Berta-Hütte, it was apparently located in the area southwest of Ravne v Bohinju; according to some local sources, "Berta-Hütte" was the old name of the current "Orožnova koča na Planini za Liscem pod Črno prstjo" hut. However, German sources indicate that in June 1943, a Zollgrenzschutz-Höhenstützpunkt was based at the "DAV gehörend Rindlerhütte (Orožen-Schutzhütte)," which was located 4 kilometers southwest of Bohinjska Bistrica.

In any case, it seems that the outpost, ransacked in 1943 and subsequently set on fire by the partisans in 1944, probably had the function of monitoring the border crossing of Baško sedlo / Vrh Bače (or Rindloch, known by the Italians as Forcella del Bove) and the Čez Suho pass on Mount Črna prst (Monte Nero di Piedicolle). It appears reasonable to assume that staff subordinated to the BZKom (G) Wocheiner-Feistritz manned some other outposts at least at the mountain pass and border crossing of Globoko (Passo Globoca) and around the current "Koča pri Triglavskih jezerih" hut (known by the Germans as "Triglavseen-Hütte"), both formerly base of a customs post of the Graničarji, but at the present day this is probably impossible to verify.

Staff subordinated to the BZKom (G) Wocheiner-Feistritz served at the *Grenzübergangsstelle* located in the complex of the railway station of Bohinjska Bistrica and in charge for the railway traffic of the border crossing of the Wocheiner-Tunnel (Bohinjski predor, which connected the Kreis Radmannsdorf with the Provincia di Gorizia). Insufficiently detailed sources also indicate the presence of Zollgrenzschutz personnel at the village rectory and at the Hotel "Markež" (currently Gostilna "Črna prst"); it has not, however, been possible to confidently link these border guards with any of the aforementioned *Dienststelle*.

Finally, the BZKom (G) Thörl-Maglern, on whose subordination the information is particularly confusing, deserves a separate discussion, since in early 1945 it seems that it had been temporarily integrated, together with some of its *Dienststelle*, under an unknown form, into the organizational structure of the BZKom (G) Wocheiner-Feistritz (see later).[14]

The town of Bohinjska Bistrica (Slovenia). In the foreground is the railway station complex that housed the headquarters of the BZKom (G) Wocheiner-Feistritz, a *Grenzübergangsstelle*, and a *Grenzzollstelle*. On the mountain crest in the background, part of the Julian Alps range, ran the Reichsgrenze sector between Mounts Vogel and Črna prst.

Bohinjsko jezero (Slovenia). The "Wocheinersee" with the church of Sv. Janez and, at the end of the lake, the settlement of Ukanc. On the mountain crest in the background, part of the Julian Alps range, ran the Reichsgrenze sector between the pass of Bogatinsko sedlo and Mount Vogel.

"Dom na Komni" hut (Ukanc, Slovenia), summer 1943. A large patrol of the Zollgrenzschutz, identifiable as the Jagdkommando des Zollgrenzschutzes Wocheiner-Feistritz, near the "Komna-Haus" during an action. The caption on the back of the photo says "BZKom (G) Kellerer." © *Author's archive*

"Dom na Komni" hut (Ukanc, Slovenia), summer 1943. The BZKom (G) Wocheiner-Feistritz, Zollinspektor Kellerer, during the same action, near the "Komna-Haus." The ruined structure had been burned by partisans during the same period. © *Author's archive*

Locality of Bogatinsko sedlo (Ukanc, Slovenia), 1942–43. Border guards belonging to the Höhenstützpunkt Bogatin-Sattel posing along with civilians and members of the Italian Guardia alla Frontiera and Guardia di Finanza of the "Distaccamento di Passo Bogatin," near the border stone nr. 16. Note the sentry box, which by now has disappeared. © *Author's archive*

Petrovo Brdo (Slovenia). The "sottotenente Ennio Poggiolini" barracks of the Guardia di Finanza, later headquarters of the GASt Petersberg. © *Tolminski Muzej*

3.1.6
The Bezirkszollkommissariat (G) Thörl-Maglern

The BZKom (G) Thörl-Maglern was probably located in Thörl-Maglern (Kreis Villach); however, most of the information about its structure is fragmentary and contradictory. It is known that between May 1939 and July 1944, the ZASt (G) Thörl-Maglern, a post subordinated to the HZA Villach—initially through the BZKom (G) Arnoldstein and later through the BZKom (G) Kronau—was based in the village; later the ZASt (G) Thörl-Maglern probably changed its designation to GASt Thörl-Maglern. At least starting from October 1944, the position of *Abteilungsführer* in Thörl-Maglern was created. It was probably also located in the village and acted as a liaison between the BZKom (G) Kronau and few *Dienststelle* directly subordinated to the *Abteilungsführer* in Thörl-Maglern, among which were at least the GASt Feistritz and der Gail and Thörl-Maglern, the outposts and warehouses belonging to the Ausweichlager des Zollgrenzschutzes Villach in Töbring and the Stützpunkt Mallestig. Finally, in November 1944 the BZKom (G) Thörl-Maglern was established within the BefSt des Zollgrenzschutzes Villach; also referred to as "Grenzschutz–BZKom (G) Thörl-Maglern," it probably took over the functions of the *Abteilungsführer* in Thörl-Maglern and integrated in its own organizational structure all the *Dienststelle* previously subordinated to the latter. As recalled earlier, in late 1944–early 1945, the BZKom (G) Thörl-Maglern was subordinated to the Abteilung Zollgrenzschutz Kärnten in Lienz through the BefSt des Zollgrenzschutzes Lienz (previously HZA Lienz). As of December 1944 the position of BZKom (G) Thörl-Maglern was held by an officer named Egger, while his deputy was apparently Hilfszollassistent Stöckl; during the same period, Zollsekretär Zigoutz apparently acted as Beamte z.b.V. The subsequent evolution of this commissariat is very confusing. Probably in view of its imminent dissolution, it seems that the BZKom (G) Thörl-Maglern was subordinated as a temporary measure—again through the BefSt des Zollgrenzschutzes Villach—to the Abteilung Zollgrenzschutz Oberkrain in Krainburg. The information in this regard is not clear enough; it seems, however, that at this stage the BZKom (G) Thörl-Maglern was atypically integrated (it is unclear in what form) into the organizational structure of the BZKom (G) Wocheiner-Feistritz. At any rate, the BZKom (G) Thörl-Maglern had apparently been dissolved for good by early April 1945. During its existence it appears that subordinated to the BZKom (G) Thörl-Maglern had been at least the GASt Feistritz an der Gail, Seltschach, and Thörl-Maglern; the Ausweichlager des Zollgrenzschutzes Villach in Töbring; and the Stützpunkt Mallestig. However, the information related to these *Dienststelle* during the last weeks of the war is particularly scarce. The following are the only data found.

The GASt Feistritz an der Gail was probably based in Feistritz an der Gail (Kreis Villach). Formerly an integral part of the organizational structure of the BZKom (G) Kronau, from December 1944 it was subordinated to the BZKom (G) Thörl-Maglern, remaining active at least until late January 1945. It was also rarely indicated as ZASt (G) Feistritz an der Gail. At least in late 1944, but likely also during the previous years, part of the organizational structure of this post was the Höhenstützpunkt Feistritzer Alm, which was based in the locality of Feistrizer Alm.

The GASt Seltschach was probably based in Seltschach (Kreis Villach). It was certainly active in November 1944; however, nothing is known about its organizational structure. Also known as GASt Thörl-Maglern/Seltschach, it is possible that it was actually the same post indicated as GASt Thörl-Maglern.

The GASt Thörl-Maglern was most likely located in Thörl-Maglern and, as already mentioned, probably coincided with the post previously known as ZASt (G) Thörl-Maglern. It seems possible that in December 1944, the post, having taken its headquarters in Seltschach, changed its name, perhaps temporarily, to GASt Thörl-Maglern/Seltschach. In any case, at the end of January 1945 the position of *Aufsichtsführender Beamter* at the GASt Thörl-Maglern was held by Zollsekretär Oberhaus, previously *Postenführer* of GASt Wocheiner-Feistritz-West. It is likely that this post remained active until the end of the war.

Regarding the Stützpunkt Mallestig, probably located in Mallestig (Kreis Villach), it was certainly still active in January 1945; it is likely that it coincided with the *Dienststelle* previously known as ZASt (G) Mallestig, but no further information is available in this regard. As for the Ausweichlager des Zollgrenzschutzes Villach in Töbring, it is dealt with in a specific paragraph.

The BZKom (G) Thörl-Maglern also provided seconded staff for the *Grenzübergangsstelle* (border-crossing point) of Coccau/Thörl (between Kreis Villach and Provincia di Udine), on which, however, no detailed information is available.[15]

3.1.7
Other *Dienststelle*

Part of the organizational structure of the HZA Villach in the city of Villach were also two *Dienststelle* in charge for taxes matters only: they were the BZKom (St) Villach, which was active between 1939 and 1944 and located in Khevenhüllergasse nr. 22, and the ZASt (St) Villach, active at least in 1939, about which no additional information was found.[16]

Furthermore, subordinated to the HZA Villach were also some customs suboffices; they were the Zollamt Arnoldstein, Assling, Ratschach-Matten, Villach, Wocheiner-Feistritz, and apparently Thörl-Maglern. Since information about these suboffices is almost nonexistent, nothing certain is known about their structure, their size, and their direct subordination.

The Zollamt Arnoldstein was located in Arnoldstein (Kreis Villach); it was active at least from late 1941–early 1942 and was led by a Vorsteher des Zollamts Arnoldstein. It was most likely the same suboffice also indicated as Eisenbahnzollamt Arnoldstein or Zollamt (Bahnhof) Arnoldstein. This suboffice hypothetically functioned as *Grenzzollstelle* at the railway station of the town, which was in charge for the railway traffic of the border crossing of Coccau/Thörl (between Kreis Villach and Provincia di Udine) and where also Grenzpolizei personnel was apparently based.

The Zollamt Assling was based in Adolf-Hitler-Straße in Jesenice (Kreis Radmannsdorf) and was active at least from mid-1941 to early 1944. It was formed by two officers and according to one source it was led by "Sekretär" Weber.

The Zollamt Ratschach-Matten was most likely based along the current Road 202 in the area of Rateče-Planica (Kreis Radmannsdorf) and was active at least from the spring of 1942, when it was apparently subordinated to the BZKom (G) Arnoldstein. It was the same suboffice also indicated as Zollamt Ratschach-Matten (L) and, in late 1943, as Straßenzollamt Ratschach-Matten, which was manned by two border guards and placed under the command of Oberzollsekretär Severin Angerer. This suboffice hypothetically functioned as a *Grenzzollstelle* at the border crossing of Fusine/Rateče (between Kreis Radmannsdorf and Provincia di Udine), where also Grenzpolizei personnel was apparently based.

The Zollamt Villach was apparently located at the railway station of that city, active at least in late 1941, and it was also indicated as Zollamt (Bahnhof) Villach.

The Zollamt Wocheiner-Feistritz, also known as Zollamt Feistritz-Wocheinersee, was located in Bohinjska Bistrica (Kreis Radmannsdorf), and it was active at least from late 1941. Led by a Vorsteher des Zollamts Wocheiner-Feistritz in mid-1944, it was run by Zollsekretär Josef Rüth. This suboffice hypothetically functioned as a *Grenzzollstelle* at the village railway station, which was in charge for the railway traffic of the border crossing of the Wocheiner-Tunnel (Bohinjski predor, which connected the Kreis Radmannsdorf with the Provincia di Gorizia) and where also Grenzpolizei personnel were apparently based.

Since, during 1943, a *Grenzzollstelle* was certainly located at the border crossing of Coccau/Thörl (between Kreis Villach and Provincia di Udine), where also Grenzpolizei personnel were based, it is conceivable that such designation indicated the Zollamt Thörl-Maglern, which was active at least in 1939, but information on this particular matter is unclear.

As for a *Zollamt* hypothetically located in Radovljica (Kreis Radmmansdorf), it is known only that, in late 1942, was active and the position of Vorsteher des Finanzamts Radmannsdorf, which was held by Steueramtmann Maier, so its existence remains unverified.[17]

More *Dienststelle* were certainly part of the organizational structure of the HZA Villach, but nothing could be found so far about their existence during the years 1941–1945. Just as an example, at least prior to the invasion of Yugoslavia some high-altitude outposts such as the Höhenstützpunkt Bresoutz, Höhenstützpunkt Mallestiger Alm, Höhenstützpunkt Panier, and Stützpunkt Pridou were based along the "Karawankengrenze" line. All of them were located in the area between Arnoldstein and Alt-Finkenstein (Kreis Villach), but nothing is known about their exact subordination and their activities after the shift of the Reichsgrenze in the Kreis Radmannsdorf.[18]

3.2
The Jagdkommando des Zollgrenzschutzes of the Hauptzollamt Villach

At least between June 1943 and August 1944, at the BZKom (G) Wocheiner-Feistritz a *Jagdkommando* ("hunting commando") was active. It was specialized in fighting partisan units and created by bringing together the most-expert border guards available at this commissariat. The command of this unit, known as Jagdkommando Wocheiner-Feistritz and formed by around forty border guards, was entrusted to Zollsekretär Johann Walz, already *Postenführer* of GASt Mitterdorf in Wochein. The unit was apparently based at the schools in Bohinjska Bistrica.

A Jagdkommando des Zollgrenzschutzes was also subordinated to the *Abteilungsführer* in Meistern. During 1943, the unit was known as Einsatzgruppe Meistern. At least in August 1943, the commander of this unit was apparently Zollsekretär Max Exner. Starting in the following autumn, members of the unit, meanwhile renamed Jagdkommando Meistern, were deployed at least temporarily with watch duties at the Höhenstützpunkt Mojstrovkapass. In February 1944, the unit consisted of one officer and thirty border guards, and its command had been entrusted to Zollsekretär Alfons Dolschein. The Jagdkommando Meistern remained active at least until July 1944.

Finally, at least from the end of November 1944, in the Faak am See area (Kreis Villach) a unit known as Zolljagdzug Mallestig ("customs hunting platoon" Mallestig) was active, probably set up within the Stützpunkt Mallestig.[19]

3.3
The Ausbildungslager and the Ausweichlager des Zollgrenzschutzes

At least since March 1942, subordinated to the HZA Villach, apparently through the BZKom (G) Arnoldstein, was a training camp referred to as Ausbildungslager des Zollgrenzschutzes Ratschach-Matten, based in the area of Rateče-Planica (Kreis Radmannsdorf); nothing is known regarding the activities of this camp. These are the only data found regarding an Ausbildungslager des Zollgrenzschutzes subordinated to the HZA Villach.

Nevertheless, at least starting from late 1941, a considerable number of border guards from the HZA Villach were trained at the Ausbildungslager des Zollgrenzschutzes Schloss Kreuthberg, a training camp based in Grad Krumperk (Kreis Stein in Oberkrain), subordinated to the HZA Krainburg, and commanded by Lagerführer Stanglmair, who was later assigned as *Postenführer* of GASt Meistern. In May 1943, the Ausbildungslager Kreuthberg was visited by the *Reichsminister der Finanzen*, Graf Schwerin von Krosigk, in the occasion of his trip to the Oberkrain.

Between 1944 and 1945, a very large number of border guards subordinated to the HZA Villach took part in specialization courses organized at the Ausbildungslager des Zollgrenzschutzes Schloss Neustein bei Lichtenwald (see later); this was a Zollgrenzschutz training camp based in Grad Impoljca (Untersteiermark), originally located in the nearby town of Raka and known as Ausbildungslager des Zollgrenzschutzes Arch and subordinated to the HZA Cilli (later BefSt des Zollgrenzschutzes Cilli / Abteilung Zollgrenzschutz Untersteiermark in Cilli). At least starting from early 1944, the Zollgrenzschutz-Ausbildungskompanie Schloss Neustein, which included some border guards from the HZA Villach, was active within this camp.

During the spring of 1945, border guards under the BZKom (G) Thörl-Maglern were trained in the village of Rattendorf (Kreis Hermagor) at an unknown facility; such training courses were probably organized by the BefSt des Zollgrenzschutzes Lienz / Abteilung Zollgrenzschutz Kärnten in Lienz.

Near Treffen am Ossiacher See (Kreis Villach), the Ausweichlager des Zollgrenzschutzes Villach in Töbring was based, a supply camp commanded, from early October 1944, by Zollsekretär Heinrich Killian, who acted as *Postenführer*; his deputy was Hilfszollassistent Köchel. In October 1944, the camp was subordinated, through the *Abteilungsführer* in Thörl-Maglern, to the BZKom (G) Kronau. Later directly subordinated to the BZKom (G) Thörl-Maglern, at least from February–March 1945, it was apparently integrated into the organizational structure of the Abteilung Zollgrenzschutz Oberkrain in Krainburg through the BZKom (G) Wocheiner-Feistritz and remained active until late April 1945. Considered as very important and strongly manned, it seems that the *Ausweichlager* was protected by some outposts, one of them apparently referred to as Stützpunkt des Zollgrenzschutzes Villach in Töbring. The *Ausweichlager* included a clothing warehouse, a *Waffenkammer* (armory), a *Munitionslager* (ammo depot), and a *Gerätlager* (equipment depot).

In February 1944, a clothing and equipment warehouse referred to as Nebenlager beim HZA Villach (subcamp at the HZA Villach) already was active, at the headquarters of the HZA Villach at 10. Oktoberstrasse nr. 11; it is likely that this camp was part of the structure of the Ausweichlager des Zollgrenzschutzes Villach in Töbring. The same applies to the very small subcamp known as Nebenlager beim Eisenbahnzollamt Arnoldstein.

Furthermore, just for completeness, it can be reported that in February 1945, within the Abteilung Zollgrenzschutz Oberkrain in Krainburg, the Ausweichlager des Zollgrenzschutzes Klagenfurt was also active, about which no additional information was found with the exception that apparently this camp had a *Waffenkammer* in the village of Ferlach (Kreis Klagenfurt).[20]

CHAPTER 4
Training and Specialization Courses

Particularly during the last months of the war, a large number of border guards subordinated to the BZKom (G) Kronau, Thörl-Maglern, and Wocheiner-Feistritz were sent to attend some training and specialization courses, on which detailed information is available.

In June 1943, for example, as ordered by the BdO Alpenland, most of the *Dienststelle* of the Zollgrenzschutz based in the Oberkrain and Untersteiermark were equipped with *Leuchtbombenmörser* (illuminating grenade launchers); hence, in the following August, border guards of the Jagdkommando des Zollgrenzschutzes Meistern took part in a training course, organized by the Gebirgs-Nebelwerfer-Lehr-und-Ausbildungs-Batterie 6, based in Bohinjska Bela (Kreis Radmannsdorf), to learn how to use grenade launchers.

In February–April 1944, members of the GASt Wocheiner-Feistritz-Nord took part in the Alpine courses organized by the Zollgrenzschutz-Hochgebirgsschule Jamtalhütte (high-mountain school of the Zollgrenzschutz Jamtalhütte), located on the Silvretta mountain range (Reichsgau Tirol und Voralberg).

In March 1944, members of the GASt Zarz took part in a *Luftmeldungdienst* (course for the air communications service) held at the Ausbildungslager des Zollgrenzschutzes Gosdorf (Reichsgau Steiermark). In August 1944, again, border guards of the BZKom (G) Kronau took part in an *Einführungslehrgang* (introductory course for post commanders) at the aforementioned Zollgrenzschutz-Ausbildungskompanie Schloss Neustein, based at the Ausbildungslager des Zollgrenzschutzes Schloss Neustein in Grad Impoljca (Untersteiermark).

At the beginning of October 1944, the *Grenzreferent* of the BdS Salzburg in Graz ordered, through the HZA Villach, that some border guards subordinated to the BZKom (G) Wocheiner-Feistritz were to participate in the *1. Führer- u. Unterführerlehrgang* (first course for officers and noncommissioned officers) at the Bandenkampfschule Kloster Sittich (the school for antiguerrilla training of Stična in the Provinz Laibach, also indicated as Bandenkampfschule HSSPF of Rösener's Führungsstab für Bandenbekämpfung). Also in October 1944, the Vorsteher des HZA Villach, Zollrat Rapf, ordered Zollsekretär Max Exner, *Postenführer* of GASt Wocheiner-Feistritz-West, to attended a four-week course at the Bandenkampfschule Sittich; Exner was apparently killed in action against partisans during this course (see later). In December 1944, Zollinspektor Karl Herppich, *Abteilungsführer* in Petersberg, was seconded to the Bandenkampfschule Grosslupp, a branch of the Bandenkampfschule Sittich based in Grosuplje (Provinz Laibach), where he was employed in action against the partisans, probably in the context of an antiguerrilla course carried out directly in the field; in February 1945, Herppich was ordered to take a training course also at the Bandenkampfschule Sittich.

Between March and April 1945, Zollsekretär Bartheloff and Stelzer, respectively *Postenführer* of the GASt Wocheiner-Feistritz and Petersberg, were sent to the Ausbildungslager des Zollgrenzschutzes Schloss Neustein to take part in a *Postenführerlehrgang für Bandenkampf* (counterguerrilla course for post commanders); Stelzer apparently went missing in action during this period.

Some vague information was also found relating to the participation of border guards of the BZKom (G) Wocheiner-Feistritz to other courses during 1945; among these were a *Funklehrgang bei Pol. Nachr. Kp. Veldes* (radio operator course at the police communication company of Bled), a *Pionierlehrgang beim Pol. Regt. Todt in Krainburg* (pioneer course at the SS-Polizei-Regiment 28 "Todt" in Kranj), and a *Gruppenführerlehrgang* (course for squad leaders) at the Ausbildungslager des Zollgrenzschutzes Schloss Neustein. Finally, in 1945, at least one border guard subordinated to the BZKom (G) Wocheiner-Feistritz took part in a training course at the *Stammkompanie* of the SS-Sipo-Ausbildungs-und-Ersatz-Bataillon Fürstenberg, commanded by SS-Untersturmführer Zimmermann; this company was indicated as subordinate to the Sipo-Schule Fürstenberg, a school formed in 1941, on the basis of the Grenzpolizeischule Pretzsch an der Elbe (Provinz Sachsen). It is interesting to note that these courses were apparently held until the last week of the war.[1]

CHAPTER 5
Zollhund and *Zollhundeführer*

At least in 1944–1945, but likely already during the previous years, by order of the Vorsteher des HZA Villach, Zollrat Rapf, training courses for the *Zollhund* (customs-duty dogs) were organized. Data in this regard are very confusing, in any case, as for the *Dienststelle* covered by this study, these courses were apparently held in Mojstrana (Kreis Radmannsdorf) for the GASt Meistern, Kronau, and Ratschach-Matten; in Latschach-Ledenitzen (Kreis Villach) for the GASt Feistritz an der Gail and Thörl-Maglern; in Bohinjska Bistrica (Kreis Radmannsdorf) for the GASt Wocheiner-Feistritz-Süd and Wocheiner-Feistritz-West; between Petrovo Brdo and Podbrdo (Provincia di Gorizia) for the GASt Zarz and the Stützpunkt Petersberg; in Rateče-Planica (Kreis Radmannsdorf) again for the GASt Meistern, Kronau, and Ratschach-Matten; and, last, in Latschach-Mallestig (Kreis Villach), again for the GASt Feistritz an der Gail and Thörl-Maglern. In addition, training reserved for puppies, conducted by the *Rüdemeister* (dog trainer) Zollsekretär Paul Müller, probably was held at the Übungslager für Zollhunde, apparently based in the area of Ulica Alojza Rabiča in Mojstrana (Kreis Radmannsdorf).

In March 1944, members of the GASt Kronau took part in a *Lehrgang für Zollhundeführer* (course for customs-duty dog handlers) at the Ausbildungslager des Zollgrenzschutzes Schloss Neustein of Grad Impoljca (Untersteiermark).

Furthermore, in spring 1945, some border guards subordinated to the BZKom (G) Wocheiner-Feistritz were sent to Salzburg (Reichsgau Salzburg) at the Hundeersatz-und-Ausbildungsstaffel-Abteilung 181, where they attended some courses, including a *Meldehundlehrgang* (training on dispatch-carrying dogs).

In February 1945, there were under the BZKom (G) Wocheiner-Feistritz five *Zollhund*: "Bussi" and "Susi" at the GASt Wocheiner-Feistritz (entrusted to Hilfszollassistent Schellander), "Tasso" at the GASt Petersberg (Zollsekretär Stelzer), and "Peter" and "Afan" at the GASt Zarz (respectively, Hilfszollassistent Pfarr and Hilfszollbetriebsassistent Saje); it is also known that the *Zollhund* "Falko" was at the GASt Kronau (Zollsekretär Pfister), while "Elsta" was at the GASt Thörl-Maglern (Hilfszollbetriebsassistent and Zollhundeführer Hauptmann).[1]

CHAPTER 6
War and Service Merit Awards

In recognition of their efforts, a fair number of members of the Zollgrenzschutz subordinated to the HZA Villach / BefSt des Zollgrenzschutzes Villach received awards for war or service merits. The following are the only data found in this regard.

Between 1940 and 1943, some border guards from the HZA Villach were awarded with the Zollgrenzschutz-Ehrenzeichen (Service Award of the Zollgrenzschutz), among them the BZKom (G) Arnoldstein Friedrich Gebhardt, Zollinspektor Arno Schott, who apparently acted as Gebhardt's adjutant, Zollsekretär Paul Müller, who was dog trainer in Mojstrana, and Zollassistent Heinrich Kreuz, fallen on June 10, 1944 (see later).

Between 1942 and 1943 the Oberkommando des Heeres proposed a substantial number of men subordinated to the Oberfinanzpräsidium Graz for awarding of the Kriegsverdienstkreuz II Klasse mit Schwertern (War Merit Cross of Second Class with Swords). For 1942, such proposals were made on January 30, April 20, and September 1, while for 1943, on January 30 and September 1. Among the various men proposed were the Grenzreferent Graz, Regierungsrat Friedrich Sperling; the Vorsteher des HZA Villach, Regierungsrat Hans-Joachim Rathke; the BZKom (G) Arnoldstein, Friedrich Gebhardt; the BZKom (G) Veldes, Anton Frischmann; the Beamte z.b.V. at the BZKom (G) Wocheiner-Feistritz, Zollsekretär Friedrich Gröschel; the *Postenführer* respectively of the ZASt (G) Althammer (Zollsekretär Heinrich Ziegler), ZASt (G) Mitterdorf in Wochein (Zollassistent Johann Walz; apparently proposed in 1944 also for the Kriegsverdienstkreuz I Klasse mit Schwertern), ZASt (G) Ratschach-Matten-Süd (Zollsekretär Heinrich Ibler), ZASt (G) Wocheiner-Feistritz (Zollassistent Rudolf Eberle as well as Zollinspektor Arno Schott, who apparently acted as adjutant of the BZKom (G) Arnoldstein), and Zollsekretär Michael Moser, who seems to have held the position of *Postenführer* of ZASt (G) Thörl-Maglern. Also proposed were five border guards of the ZASt (G) Althammer, five of the ZASt (G) Meistern, three of the ZASt (G) Kronau, nine of the ZASt (G) Mitterdorf in Wochein, two of the ZASt (G) St. Johann am Wocheinersee, three of the ZASt (G) Wocheiner-Feistritz, and one of the ZASt (G) Ratschach-Matten.

On December 8, 1944, thirteen border guards subordinated to the BZKom (G) Wocheiner-Feistritz were proposed for the Kriegsverdienstkreuz II Klasse mit Schwertern; they were the *Abteilungsführer* in Petersberg, Zollinspektor Karl Herppich; two members of the *Stab* of the BZKom (G) Wocheiner-Feistritz; three of the GASt Wocheiner-Feistritz-West; two of the GASt Wocheiner-Feistritz-Süd; four of the GASt Petersberg; and one of the GASt Zarz (a Hilfswilliger from Spodnje Danje, Kreis Krainburg).

Last, on March 15, 1945, Zollinspektor Herppich, representing the BZKom (G) Wocheiner-Feistritz, proposed for the same award thirteen border guards subordinated to the BZKom (G) Wocheiner-Feistritz; one belonged to the *Stab* of the BZKom (G) Wocheiner-Feistritz, one to the GASt Wocheiner-Feistritz, six to the GASt Wocheiner-Feistritz-West, three to the GASt Petersberg, and two to the GASt Zarz (including one Hilfswilliger from Sorica, Kreis Krainburg).

On March 28, 1945, Rösener awarded, through the Abteilung Zollgrenzschutz Oberkrain in Krainburg, nine Kriegsverdienstkreuz II Klasse mit Schwertern; of these, six were assigned to border guards from the BZKom (G) Kronau, and three to men subordinated to the BZKom (G) Wocheiner-Feistritz. The awarding was accompanied by personal congratulations from Rösener and the BdS Salzburg, SS-Brigadeführer Schulz. Among the border guards awarded on that occasion there was also the *Abteilungsführer* in Petersberg, Zollinspektor Herppich; he had joined the Reichsfinanzverwaltung in 1936 and had been on duty in the Oberkrain since 1941.

In addition, in 1944 at least one border guard of the GASt Petersberg was apparently proposed for the award of the Eisernes Kreuz II Klasse (Iron Cross of Second Class), but no additional information was found in this regard.

Given the intense antipartisan activity conducted by the men of the Zollgrenzschutz located in the Oberkrain, some of them were almost certainly awarded, by the Führungsstab für Bandenbekämpfung of Rösener, the "infamous" Bandenkampfabzeichen (Antipartisan Combat Badge). The only document found in this regard related to border guards active under the territorial jurisdiction of the HZA Villach / BefSt des Zollgrenzschutzes Villach is the *Bandenkampftagenliste* (list of participation in days of combat against the partisans) of Zollinspektor Rudolf Schaffer, who, in July 1944, requested the accreditation of six *Bandenkampftage* accumulated during his own previous service at the BZKom (G) Wocheiner-Feistritz in the bitter clashes that took place in the Provincia di Gorizia near Novaki in April 1944 and Podbrdo in June–July 1944 (see later).[1]

CHAPTER 7
Previous Service in Other Military Corps and Transfers to Other Units

A fair number of border guards subordinated to the HZA Villach had previously served in other armed forces. There were many veterans of the First World War, as members both of the German and Austro-Hungarian armies, some of whom had also received awards. Some others had taken part in the Kärntner Abwehrkampf (Austro-Yugoslav conflict in Carinthia of 1919), such as, for instance, the Vorsteher des HZA Villach, Zollrat Rapf. Some others, after participating in the First World War in the Austro-Hungarian army, had served in the "ehemalige Jugoslawische Finanzverwaltung" (in this case to be understood as the Yugoslav border guards generically known as Graničarji) over the 1920s–1930s. There were also men of South Tyrolean origin who had served in the Italian Royal Army during the 1920s–1930s. A representative example was an ethnic Slovenian born in 1893 in Bohinjska Bistrica, who took part in the fighting in Carinthia in 1919 as a member of the Yugoslav army: enlisted in 1920 in a Graničarji unit ("Finanz-Verwaltungsdienst des Königsreich Jugoslavien") based in Rateče-Planica, he joined the Zollamt Ratschach-Matten in 1941; according to his memoirs, after the war, he was initially reinstated in the Graničarji of Tito's Yugoslavia in Bohinjska Bistrica and later forced to expatriate to Austria since he was accused by the OZNA (Yugoslav secret services) of being a Volksdeutscher.

Following the Italian armistice with the Allies on September 8, 1943, an unknown number of members of the Italian Guardia di Finanza were also integrated into the structure of the BZKom (G) Kronau; these men, who at least initially were allowed to keep their uniform, wore the green armbands with the obsolete *Wappenschild* (numbered identification badge) already in use by the auxiliary staff of the Zollgrenzschutz until the early 1940s.[1]

In December 1944, following an order by Himmler, a unit called Einsatzgruppe Oberrhein was constituted in Donaueschingen (Land Baden); also indicated as Einsatzgruppe "Grenzschutz" in Donaueschingen, it numbered fourteen battalions formed of members of the Zollgrenzschutz made available by their own BZKom (G). Deployed near the fortified lines along the Franco-German border, these battalions were employed in combat, suffering heavy casualties.

Between December 1944 and February 1945, by order of the *Grenzreferent* of the BdS Salzburg in Graz, personnel subordinated to the Abteilung Zollgrenzschutz Oberkrain in Krainburg, including border guards belonging to the GASt Petersberg, Zarz, and Wocheiner-Feistritz-West, were transferred to Grad Impoljca and Krško (Untersteiermark) to create the 1. Einsatzkompanie Donaueschingen–Zollgrenzschutzeinsatzgruppe Oberrhein. This company, also known as Einsatzkompanie Arch and apparently based in Raka (Untersteiermark), was placed under the command of Zollinspektor Max Nelde, previously BZKom (G) St. Martin (HZA Krainburg). It remains unclear exactly to which Zollgrenzschutz headquarters this company was subordinated, perhaps to the BefSt des Zollgrenzschutzes Arch. In any case, it seems that was set up within the training area of the Ausbildungslager des Zollgrenzschutzes Schloss Neustein and later transferred to the Hindenburg-Kaserne in Donaueschingen, where it was subordinated to the Leiter der Einsatzgruppe Oberrhein, Oberregierungsrat Penndorf, previously Leiter des Zollgrenzschutzes Südost (Serbien).

At the end of December 1944, the *Grenzreferent* of the BdS Salzburg in Graz arranged, through the Leiter der BefSt des Zollgrenzschutzes Villach, the transfer of some border guards belonging to the GASt Wocheiner-Feistritz, for a period of six to eight months, to a department designated as Rüstungsstab Kammler Kohlerbergbau Seegraben (armaments headquarters Kammler of the coal mine Seegraben), probably based in Leoben (Reichsgau Steiermark).

Finally, in March 1945, some border guards subordinated to the BZKom (G) Wocheiner-Feistritz, including some local *Hilfswilliger*, were apparently transferred at first to the Oberkrainer Selbstschutz (self-defense militia of the Oberkrain) and later to some Waffen-SS unit within the SS-Ergänzungsstelle XVIII Alpenland in Salzburg (Hellbrunner-Kaserne). Furthermore, late in the war, other border guards of the HZA Villach were transferred also to various Wehrmacht units, such as, for example, the Gebirgsjäger-Ersatz-und-Ausbildungs-Regiment 138 and 139, respectively based in Leoben and Villach.[2]

CHAPTER 8
Psychological Implications, Discipline, and Military Justice

The customs and border service in sparsely inhabited and particularly isolated areas such as those of the Julian Alps sector apparently had an important psychological impact on the members of the Zollgrenzschutz employed in such a duty. On the basis of the collected data, particularly alienating—perhaps because it was considered as extremely monotonous—seems to have been the duty at the *Grenzübergangsstelle* and *Höhenstützpunkt* located in rural areas, such as, for example, the Alpine passes. In practice, the psychological distress often resulted in disciplinary infringements, such as, in milder cases, arbitrary abandonment of the post during the watch duty, alcohol abuse, or illegal border trespassing, up to even extreme acts such as self-harm or suicide attempts; this, for example, was the case of a South Tyrolean *Hilfszollbetriebsassistent* who took his own life on October 31, 1944, at the headquarters of the GASt Ratschach-Matten.

Following the integration of the Zollgrenzschutz into the organizational structure of the Reichssicherheitshauptamt, the responsibility for disciplinary matters of these units was transferred to the "infamous" SS- und Polizeigericht (SS/Polizei courts), who often and willingly punished disciplinary offenses with prison sentences. However, prison sentences do not seem to have produced the desired effect, so much so that, as the end of the conflict approached, offences of a political nature also began to appear among the men of the Zollgrenzschutz; as an example, a guard subordinated to the BZKom (G) Wocheiner-Feistritz was placed under arrest at the end of December 1944, upon order of the SS- und Polizeigericht XVIII–Zweigstelle Salzburg, for acts of defeatism that occurred in Töbring (Kreis Villach).[1]

CHAPTER 9
The Antipartisan Activity of the Zollgrenzschutz Units of the Hauptzollamt Villach

Given their functions and the particularly impervious territory of deployment, largely covered by dense forests and affected by vast mountain ranges, the border guards units of the HZA Villach / BefSt des Zollgrenzschutzes Villach often found themselves involved in roundups and antipartisan operations organized both in the Oberkrain and, after the Italian armistice, in the territories belonging to the neighboring OZAK. Also in regard to operations, the available information is fragmentary and certainly incomplete; the following are the only data found on this topic.[1] Since the postwar Slovenian partisan bibliography is not always reliable in regard to this particular topic, it was decided to reconstruct these events mainly on the basis of contemporaneous documentation of German origin.

December 17, 1941: During a partisan night attack against the Zollgrenzstützpunkt Mojstrana (Kreis Radmannsdorf), a Zollgrenzschutz officer is wounded and a partisan is killed.[2]

March 13, 1942: A patrol of the ZASt (G) St. Johann am Wocheinersee captures two partisans at the "Voga-Alpe," likely to be understood as the area of the Vogar, northwest of Stara Fužina (Kreis Radmannsdorf). One of them is killed while trying to run away.[3]

July 22, 1942: Following a mass forced recruitment of the local population organized by the partisans in the locality of Gorjuše, north of Nomenj (Kreis Radmannsdorf), members of the Zollgrenzschutz, the Polizei-Skistreifen-Abteilung, the Reserve-Polizei-Bataillon 171, the Gendarmerie, and the Wehrmacht, supported by a *Panzerzug* (armored train), are sent to that area. While approaching the scattered settlement of Gorjuše, the German column, after a brief fire exchange with the partisans that put them on the run, arrests twenty-two local men. The German units then proceed to carry out a sweep, with no results, in the direction of the plateau of Pokljuka and along the Bohinj basin.[4]

July 30, 1942: Following a report on the presence of a heavily armed partisan group near Bahnwachterhaus 10 (railway guardhouse 10), a mixed patrol made up of members of the Gendarmerieposten Kronau and the Zollgrenzschutz intervenes in the area between Podkluže and Gozd Martuljek (Kreis Radmannsdorf). According to the investigations carried out on the spot by the patrol, the partisan group was responsible for an ambush on the car of SS-Obersturmführer Dr. Karl Starzacher, director of the Reichsgauarchiv Klagenfurt (currently Kärntner Landesarchiv) and *Stabsführer* of the Dienststelle des Beauftragten des Reichskommissar für die Festigung deutschen Volkstums in Veldes (head of the branch of the Reich inspector for the consolidation of the Germanic national identity located in Bled). The patrol has no contact with the enemy.[5]

August 23, 1942: A Zollgrenzschutz patrol clashes with partisans in the area of the current "Vodnikov dom na Velem polju" hut, 3 km southeast of Mount Triglav (Kreis Radmannsdorf). Three partisans are wounded and captured. Following this firefight, members of the Zollgrenzschutz, the Gendarmerie, and the Polizei-Skistreifen-Abteilung, supported by a

Pak-Zug (antitank platoon) of the Polizei-Gebirgsjäger-Regiment 18, take part in an action in the same area. During the clashes, one member of the Polizei-Skistreifen-Abteilung and two partisans are killed, and one partisan is wounded and captured.[6]

September 6–8, 1942: Members of the Zollgrenzschutz, the Gendarmerie, and the Polizei-Skistreifen-Abteilung take part in an unsuccessful operation on the plateau of Pokljuka, north of Bohinjska Bistrica (Kreis Radmannsdorf).[7]

September 11, 1942: Following the looting of foodstuffs by the partisans near Nemški Rovt (Kreis Radmannsdorf), members of the Gendarmerie assisted by border guards from the BZKom (G) Wocheiner-Feistritz are sent there to investigate. For similar reasons, members of the Gendarmerie and of a post of the Zollgrenzschutz from Kranjska Gora intervene in the locality of Gozd Martuljek (Kreis Radmannsdorf).[8]

September 14, 1942: Members of the Zollgrenzschutz and of the 7. Kompanie of the SS-Polizei-Regiment 19 intervene at the sawmills located in the settlement of Belica, near Mojstrana (Kreis Radmannsdorf), set on fire by partisans.[9]

November 9, 1942: During a firefight, border guards apparently belonging to the GASt Althammer kill a partisan in the locality of Planina Bareča dolina, near Laški Rovt (Kreis Radmannsdorf).[10]

November 26, 1942: In the late afternoon, a patrol made up of three border guards of the GASt Wocheiner-Feistritz falls into a partisan ambush in the area of the "Menzinger" farm (probably to be identified with the current "Mencingerjeva Koča" hut), near Ravne v Bohinju (Kreis Radmannsdorf). The patrol commander, Hilfszollassistent Miggitsch, is killed while two *Hilfszollbetriebsassistent*, one of whom slightly injured, manage to return to their post to give the alarm. A second patrol of the post, led by Zollsekretär Richter, immediately sent from the post to the scene of the firefight to retrieve the body of Miggitsch, subsequently sweeps the area without success; border guards of the Höhenstützpunkt Berta-Hütte and members of the Gendarmerieposten Wocheiner-Feistritz also take part to this reconnaissance.[11]

May 12, 1943: Members of the Zollgrenzschutz are employed in action as support for a patrol of the Gendarmerie severely attacked by partisans in the area of Nomenj (Kreis Radmannsdorf).[12]

June 5, 1943: In the context of a vaster operation, members of the Zollgrenzschutz set up a *Lauerstellung* (ambush blockade) between Bohinjska Bistrica and Nemški Rovt (Kreis Radmannsdorf), during which a partisan is killed.[13]

June 18, 1943: Members of the Zollgrenzschutz, the II. Bataillon of the SS-Polizei-Regiment 19, the Gendarmerie, and the Gebirgs-Nebelwerfer-Lehr-und-Ausbildungs-Batterie 6 take part in an unsuccessful antipartisan operation in the area south of Bohinjska Bistrica (Kreis Radmannsdorf).[14]

June 23, 1943: Members of the Zollgrenzschutz, the II. and III. Bataillon of the SS-Polizei-Regiment 19, the Gendarmerie-Reserve-Kompanie (mot.) "Alpenland" 2 and 3, the Polizei-Kompanie z.b.V. "Alpenland," and the Polizei-Gebirgsjäger-Kompanie "Alpenland" take part in an antipartisan operation in the Bohinj basin (Kreis Radmannsdorf); a partisan is killed on Mount Javorov vrh, north of Bohinjska Češnjica.[15]

June 27, 1943: A patrol of the Zollgrenzschutz arrests a woman, suspected to be a partisan, near Studor v Bohinju (Kreis Radmannsdorf).[16]

July 2, 1943: A patrol of the Zollgrenzschutz clashes with the partisans on Mount Rudnica, near the village of Brod in the Bohinj basin (Kreis Radmannsdorf), where a partisan is slightly wounded. A subsequent joint sweep, conducted in the same area by men belonging to the

Zollgrenzschutz, the Gendarmerie, and the (mot.) Überwachungskommando of the Polizei-Gebirgsjäger-Kompanie "Alpenland," does not achieve any results. During the night of July 1–2, a large partisan group infiltrates the villages of Dovje and Mojstrana (Kreis Radmannsdorf) in search of food and attacks the headquarters of the *Abteilungsführer* in Meistern, of the Einsatzgruppe Meistern, and of the Gendarmerieposten Meistern. Members of the Zollgrenzschutz along with policemen of the Gendarmerie and the 7. Kompanie of the SS-Polizei-Regiment 19 are involved in the fighting to free the area from the partisan presence. Two members of the Zollgrenzschutz and a partisan are wounded.[17]

July 3, 1943: In the evening, members of the Zollgrenzschutz, the Gendarmerie, the Wehrmacht, the 6. Kompanie of the Polizei-Wach-Bataillon XVIII and the 7. and 10. Kompanie of the SS-Polizei-Regiment 19 take part in the sweep of the areas affected on the same day by a large antipartisan operation (*Grosseinsatz*) conducted on the Pokljuka plateau (Kreis Radmannsdorf). Such action was organized in response to firefights that had taken place on the previous day between the villages of Dovje and Mojstrana. During the action, twelve partisans are killed while another twenty are captured. The German units have one wounded and one dead, the latter being likely a member of the 7. Kompanie of the SS-Polizei-Regiment 19 killed in the area of Mount Lipanski vrh.[18]

July 11, 1943: A patrol of the GASt Althammer shoots down an "*englischer Störballon*" (British explosive balloon) in the locality of Voje, near Stara Fužina (Kreis Radmannsdorf).[19]

August 2–4, 1943: Three hundred border guards from the HZA Krainburg and Villach, along with members of the Polizei-Kompanie z.b.V. "Alpenland," the Polizei-Gebirgsjäger-Kompanie "Alpenland," the II. and III. Bataillon of the SS-Polizei-Regiment 19, the Gendarmerie-Reserve-Kompanie (mot.) "Alpenland" 2 and 3, and the Gendarmerieposten Oberdorf take part in a large antipartisan operation (*Grosseinsatz*) held astride the Reichsgrenze in the area of Žiri (Kreis Krainburg). In this context, forty border guards of the BZKom (G) Wocheiner-Feistritz are deployed along the line Selo-Gorenja vas. On August 9, the BdO Alpenland, Generalmajor der Polizei Brenner, sends for information to the Vorsteher des HZA Villach, Zollrat Rapf, a report on the results obtained by the operation.[20]

September 16, 1943: On order from the BdO Alpenland, Generalmajor der Polizei Brenner, an antipartisan operation is organized with the aim of stopping the partisan units stationed in the Bohinj basin (Kreis Radmannsdorf) from smuggling explosives in the Provincia di Gorizia. The task is to identify a partisan warehouse in an area located 3.5 km northeast of Bohinjska Bistrica (identifiable with the locality of Koprivnik v Bohinju), annihilate the partisan formations in the vicinity, and arrest fifteen people wanted for belonging to a partisan support organization. Policemen of the 4. Kompanie of the Polizei-Wach-Bataillon XVII, the 5. Kompanie of the Polizei-Wach-Bataillon XVIII, the 1. Zug (Göriach) of the II. Bataillon of the SS-Polizei-Regiment 19, the (mot.) Kommando I of the Polizei-Gebirgsjäger-Kompanie "Alpenland," and the Gendarmerieposten Neuming, all placed at the orders of the commander of the 5. Kompanie of the Polizei-Wach-Bataillon XVIII, have the task of destroying, at dawn, the aforementioned warehouse and eliminating the partisan unit guarding it. Telecommunications are ensured by the Gebirgs-Polizei-Nachrichten-Kompanie 181. At the same time, eighty men of the Gendarmerie-Hauptmannschaft Krainburg, to whom forty-two border guards of the Jagdkommando des Zollgrenzschutzes Wocheiner-Feistritz are subordinated for the action, have the task, along with men of the KdS Veldes, to track down and arrest the members of the partisan support organization. Nothing is known about the course of the operation; however, fourteen wanted people are captured and imprisoned at the Strafanstalt Vigaun (the KdS Veldes prison located in Begunje).[21]

October 6, 1943: The GASt Dautscha, located in the scattered settlement of Davča (Kreis Krainburg) and at that date still subordinated to the BZKom (G) Laak-West (HZA Krainburg), is severely attacked by the partisans; during the firefight, Hilfszollbetriebsassistent Ruttnig, belonging to the post, is fatally wounded. The intervention of "Gruppe Bremken," named from Zollassistent Johann Bremken of the GASt Zarz, apparently composed of border guards from his post and from the GASt Petersberg, forces the partisans to retreat.[22]

October 9, 1943: During a private trip, Hilfszollbetriebsassistent Murhard, from the *Stab* of the BZKom (G) Wocheiner-Feistritz, is killed in a partisan ambush in Poljane, near Spodnje Gorje (Kreis Radmannsdorf).[23]

October 21, 1943: A *Hilfszollassistent* of the Jagdkommando des Zollgrenzschutzes Wocheiner-Feistritz is severely wounded by mistake by the watch post of the Grenzwacht-Kompanie Wocheiner-Feistritz in Bohinjska Bistrica (Kreis Radmannsdorf), a Heer unit. The cause of the incident was apparently a wrong password.[24]

November 11–22, 1943: In the context of Unternehmen Traufe, Zollgrenzschutz units are apparently employed in the area of Bohinjska Bistrica (Kreis Radmannsdorf), but no precise information could be found as to whether forces from the HZA Villach took part in this operation. It is known, however, that during November 21 and 22, border guards of the GASt Schwarzenberg-Ost (HZA Krainburg) are employed near the Reichsgrenze around the village of Sorica (Kreis Krainburg), an area at this time already subordinated to the HZA Villach.[25]

December 21, 1943: Antipartisan operation along the Baška grapa valley (Provincia di Gorizia) with participation of units from the Sicherungsgruppe von le Fort, including members of the Italian Battaglione Bersaglieri "Mussolini," German *Gebirgsjäger* based in Podbrdo, and border guards of the GASt Petersberg. Specifically, the border guards take part, together with the Kompanie Kefer (1. Kompanie of the Gebirgsjäger-Ersatz-und-Ausbildungs-Bataillon 139), in fighting near Nemški Rut; according to Zollgrenzschutz sources, about a hundred partisans are killed in this phase. During the operation, the Zollgrenzschutz men also seem to be involved in harsh hand-to-hand fighting with the partisans in the village of Stržišče. Furthermore, border guards of the GASt Petersberg apparently take part, together with men of the 1. Kompanie of Reserve-Gebirgsjäger-Regiment 139, in fightings in the area of Podbrdo; in the latter locality, Hilfszollbetriebsassistent Swozill from the HZA Villach is killed.[26]

January 8, 1944: A patrol of the Talstützpunkt Wurzen clashes with partisans between the village of Podkoren and the Wurzenpass/Korensko sedlo (Alpine pass between Kreis Villach and Kreis Radmannsdorf); a partisan from Kranjska Gora is killed during the firefight.[27]

January 18, 1944: A patrol of the Zollgrenzschutz based in Kranjska Gora clashes with partisans in the locality of Srednji vrh near Gozd Martuljek (Kreis Radmannsdorf). Following the fighting, a camp considered as partisan shelter is set on fire.[28]

January 23, 1944: Border guards of the GASt Petersberg and Zarz take part in an operation near Sorica (Kreis Krainburg). During the clashes with the partisans, which take place near the headquarters of the GASt Zarz, Hilfszollbetriebsassistent Rauter, who belonged to the post, is killed.[29]

March 10, 1944: During a service trip, Hilfszollbetriebsassistent Filippi, from the GASt Mitterdorf in Wochein, and Salfellner, from the GASt St. Veit (HZA Krainburg), are killed by the partisans near Grad Krumperk (Kreis Stein in Oberkrain). They both were seconded for a course at the Ausbildungslager des Zollgrenzschutzes Schloss Kreuthberg.[30]

April 9, 1944: During a trip to Žlan near Bohinjska Bistrica (Kreis Radmannsdorf), Hilfszollbetriebsassistent Schäfer from the GASt Wocheiner-Feistritz goes missing, probably kidnapped by partisans.[31]

April 16–18, 1944: In the context of the Unternehmen Wendelstein, three not-further-identified companies formed by members of the Zollgrenzschutz guard the Reichsgrenze in the area of Cerkno (Provincia di Gorizia). On April 16, border guards of the GASt Petersberg, apparently under the command of the Vorsteher des HZA Villach, Zollrat Rapf, severely clash with the partisans near Novaki (Provincia di Gorizia), inflicting some losses on them. Oberzollinspektor Kellerer (perhaps already as replacement of the BZKom (G) Kronau), Zollinspektor Schaffer (possibly as *Abteilungsführer* in Petersberg), the *Postenführer* of GASt Kronau (Zollsekretär Pfister), and the *Stützpunktführer* at Mojstrovkapass (Zollassistent Doujak) apparently participate in these fights, most likely together with subordinated staff who had arrived through the Wocheiner-Tunnel (Bohinjski predor, the railway tunnel Bohinjska Bistrica-Podbrdo, which connected the Kreis Radmannsdorf with the Provincia di Gorizia). During April 17–19, border guards subordinated to the HZA Krainburg are also involved in the area, in particular around the villages of Trata, Hotavlje, Stara Oselica, and Fužine (Kreis Krainburg). On April 19, the commander of the 188. Reserve-Gebirgs-Division, Generalleutnant von Hösslin, sends his written thanks to the Vorsteher des HZA Krainburg, Regierungsrat Hahn, for the border guards made available for these operations.[32]

Gozd Martuljek (Slovenia), April 16–18, 1944. A column formed by border guards subordinated to the BZKom (G) Kronau, on the bridge of Gozd Martuljek during Unternehmen Wendelstein. © *Kärntner Landesarchiv*

Bohinjska Bistrica (Slovenia), April 16–18, 1944. The column formed by border guards subordinated to the BZKom (G) Kronau boards the train in order to cross the Wocheiner-Tunnel during the Unternehmen Wendelstein. © *Kärntner Landesarchiv*

Podbrdo (Slovenia), April 16–18, 1944. The column, including Zollsekretär Pfister (*second from left*), arrives at the railway yard of Podbrdo during the Unternehmen Wendelstein. © *Kärntner Landesarchiv*

Unidentified location (Slovenia), April 16–18, 1944. Men of the Zollgrenzschutz guarding the first partisans captured during the Unternehmen Wendelstein. © *Kärntner Landesarchiv*

Novaki (Cerkno, Slovenia), April 16–18, 1944. The Vorsteher des HZA Villach, Zollrat Rapf (*on the right*), with Oberzollinspektor Kellerer (*in the middle*) during the Unternehmen Wendelstein. © *Kärntner Landesarchiv*

Novaki (Cerkno, Slovenia), April 16–18, 1944. The Vorsteher des HZA Villach, Zollrat Rapf (*first on the left*), and his men marching during the Unternehmen Wendelstein; note the presence of a *Zollhund* in the column. © *Kärntner Landesarchiv*

Novaki (Cerkno, Slovenia), April 16–18, 1944. Zollsekretär Pfister (*sitting*), Oberzollinspektor Kellerer (*with binoculars*), and the *Stützpunktführer* at Mojstrovkapass, Zollassistent Doujak (*in front of the entrance of the structure*), resting during Unternehmen Wendelstein. © *Author's archive*

May 5, 1944: Border guards of the GASt Petersberg capture three partisans following a clash that apparently took place at a checkpoint near the railway bridge of Bitnje, east of Bohinjska Bistrica (Kreis Radmannsdorf).[33]

May 23, 1944: Border guards of the GASt Althammer clash with a partisan unit that showed up in the area of Stara Fužina (Kreis Radmannsdorf), looking for food. After half an hour of hard fighting, the partisans withdraw. Around Srednja vas v Bohinju, probably in this context, Hilfszollsekretär Spörk, referred to as "*i. V. Postenführer GASt Althammer*," is mortally wounded.[34]

Kranj (Slovenia), May 26, 1944. The burial of Hilfszollsekretär Spörk, "*i. V. Postenführer GASt Althammer*," at the Heldenfriedhof Krainburg (the German military cemetery of Kranj). At least eleven border guards subordinated to the HZA Villach were buried there. © *Kärntner Landesarchiv*

June 3, 1944: During a partisan attack on the GASt Wocheinersee (Kreis Radmannsdorf), Hilfszollbetriebsassistent Linder is killed by shrapnel.[35]

June 10, 1944: Zollsekretär Kreuz, at least in March 1942, under the ZASt (G) Mitterdorf in Wochein, dies in Sv. Janez (Kreis Radmannsdorf). Nothing is known regarding the circumstances of his death.[36]

June 27, 1944: Members of the Zollgrenzschutz set flames to a partisan camp in the area of Kranjska Gora (Kreis Radmannsdorf).[37]

June 29, 1944: A patrol made up of fifteen border guards belonging to the GASt Wocheinersee takes part in an antipartisan action in the locality of Bogatinsko sedlo (Alpine pass and border crossing between Kreis Radmannsdorf and Provincia di Gorizia). After resting at the "Kärntner-Haus" hut (unidentified; perhaps the current "Koča pod Bogatinom"), at 14:45 the patrol is preparing to return to its post. Having arrived in the locality of Komna (to be understood as near the current "Dom na Komni" hut, known by Germans as "Komna-Haus"), the border guards are attacked by the partisans on three sides, suffering some losses. However, the patrol manages to disengage by gathering at the serpentine that leads to the locality of "Koča pri Savici" (Slap Savica), at the time apparently headquarters of the Stützpunkt Savica. At 22:00 a second patrol arrives on-site. It was sent to the scene by the BZKom (G) Wocheiner-Feistritz, with the task of assisting the wounded and recovering the bodies of the two fallen during the firefight; they were Zollsekretär Hartwich, the patrol commander, and Hilfszollbetriebsassistent Dannehl. Three more border guards are reported missing; of these, two were able to return to their post on June 30, while the third one, Hilfszollbetriebsassistent Prazdny, would never be found again.[38]

July 1–2, 1944: Members of the Zollgrenzschutz take part in an operation along the Baška Grapa valley (Provincia di Gorizia), organized to rescue units of the Italian Battaglione Bersaglieri "Mussolini" and Reggimento Alpini "Tagliamento," which had been under severe partisan attack from the previous day. On July 1, border guards subordinated to the BZKom (G) Wocheiner-Feistritz, including members of the GASt Petersberg—perhaps under the command of Zollinspektor Schaffer—participate in the fighting in the area of Podbrdo. During these clashes, losses are sustained by the Lehr-Regiment "Brandenburg," the Polizei-Gebirgsjäger-Kompanie "Alpenland," and the SS-Polizei-Regiment 28 "Todt"; these units had arrived from the Oberkrain through the Wocheiner-Tunnel (Bohinjski predor) to support the operations. Between July 1 and 2, border guards of the GASt Petersberg repel a partisan attack near Grahovo ob Bači (Provincia di Gorizia), suffering some losses.[39]

July 7(?), 1944: Border guards of the GASt Petersberg intervene to rescue the GASt Zarz (Kreis Krainburg), attacked by partisans.[40]

July 15, 1944: A *Hilfszollbetriebsassistent* from the GASt Kronau (Kreis Radmannsdorf) is severely wounded by an unknown explosive device. He loses both forearms.[41]

August 23, 1944: Members of the Zollgrenzschutz clash with a small partisan group near Mount Steinberg, 2 km east of the Wurzenpass/Korensko sedlo (Alpine pass between the Kreis Villach and Kreis Radmannsdorf). A partisan, referred to as "*Politkommissar*," is killed while the rest of his group retreats and disengages from combat.[42]

August 30, 1944: Hilfszollassistent Gössler from the GASt Wocheiner-Feistritz-West is killed during a clash with partisans in Greuth, near Faak am See (Kreis Villach). Nothing is known about the context of this fighting.[43]

September 10, 1944: Border guards of the GASt Wocheiner-Feistritz take part in an action at an unidentified location. The same day, a member of the GASt Wocheiner-Feistritz-Süd on patrol kills a partisan courier and seriously injures another.[44]

September 20–21, 1944: In the night between September 20 and 21, a large group of around two hundred partisans surround the village of Gozd Martuljek (Kreis Radmannsdorf). Four border guards of the Stützpunkt Wald along with four officers undergoing training at the Gauschule Wald (school for officers of the NSDAP), both based at the Hotel "Coop," try in vain to repel the attack. The warehouses of the Gauschule are raided by the partisans, while two members of the Zollgrenzschutz are wounded. During the night, two patrols, respectively belonging to the Gendarmerieposten Kronau and the Zollgrenzschutz, intervene and by using heavy machine guns manage to make the partisans retreat.[45]

Note: As recalled earlier, during the autumn of 1944 the HZA Villach changed its designation to BefSt des Zollgrenzschutzes Villach.

October 13, 1944: Members of the Zollgrenzschutz and the Wehrmacht conduct an action in Alt-Finkenstein (Kreis Villach) aimed at obtaining the release of the local *Bauernführer* (farmers' representative), kidnapped the day before by a large partisan group. Thanks to the operation, the partisans are dispersed and the prisoner is freed.[46]

October 14, 1944: During the morning, on order of the commander of the Sicherungsabschnitt VII (Bled), an operation is organized with all the available local units in the village of Uskovnica (Kreis Radmannsdorf). Taking part in the action are seventeen men of the "SD-Sonderkommando z.b.V.," forty-six border guards of the BZKom (G) Wocheiner-Feistritz, and twenty-one policemen from the Gendarmerieposten Neuming and Wocheiner-Feistritz. The action is carried out along the route Bohinjska Bistrica–Pkt. 503 (probably across the Sava River toward the locality of Pod Šavnikom)–603 (south of the current Senožeta ski slopes)–Srednja vas v Bohinju–Pkt. 620–1161 (probably south of the locality of Prehod)–Uskovnica. It is known that around 9:00 a.m., a *Sicherungsstreife* (security patrol) of the Zollgrenzschutz, apparently led by the BZKom (G) Wocheiner-Feistritz Walter Kasischke, is employed on the saddle between Mount Rudnica and Mount Savnica, south of Srednja vas v Bohinju. At the same time, policemen of the Gendarmerieposten Neuming with a "*Bahn-draisine*" (railway trolley) move toward Bohinjska Bistrica, where they apparently reach more border guards employed there with reconnaissance tasks. Around Pkt. 620, which apparently corresponds to the northern exit of Srednja vas v Bohinju, the *Sicherungsstreife* of the Zollgrenzschutz clashes with and destroys a partisan group armed with machine guns. Furthermore, around forty partisans are put on the run northeast of the village of Uskovnica, which is freed at 5:30 p.m. During the fighting in the latter locality, Hilfszollassistent Preiß, who belonged to the GASt Wocheiner-Feistritz-West, dies. At least two partisans are killed during the action. Perhaps in retaliation for Preiß's death, on October 20, members of the GASt Wocheiner-Feistritz-West take part again in an action in Uskovnica, during which five partisans are captured.[47]

November 2, 1944: Border guards of the GASt Zarz, including some local *Hilfswilliger*, are engaged in the defense of the village of Spodnje Danje (Kreis Krainburg), attacked by partisans.[48] On the same day, SS men run into two partisans near the SS-Erholungsheim (sanatorium of the SS) based at the Hotel "Erika" in the locality of Velika Pišnica, a valley between Kranjska Gora and the border crossing of Prelaz Vršič (Kreis Radmannsdorf). One of the partisans is captured, while the other, after a brief firefight, manages to escape in the direction of Kranjska Gora. In the following hours, members of the Zollgrenzschutz stationed in Kranjska Gora, assisted by a patrol of the Gendarmerieposten Kronau, set up an ambush blockade and sweep the area in search of the fugitive.[49]

November 3, 1944: Hilfszollassistent Laber, who belonged to the Talstützpunkt Wurzen, is killed in a partisan ambush apparently during a patrol service in Podkoren (Kreis Radsmanndorf). During the firefight, an *Hilfszollbetriebsassistent* is also seriously wounded.[50]

Kranjska Gora (Slovenia), current Borovška cesta nr. 27, November 6, 1944. The mortuary of Hilfszollassistent Laber inside the "Hoßfeld-Haus," headquarters of the BZKom (G) Kronau. Laber, who belonged to the Talstützpunkt Wurzen, was killed by partisans in an ambush in Podkoren on November 3, 1944. © *Kärntner Landesarchiv*

Kranjska Gora (Slovenia), current Borovška cesta nr. 27, November 6, 1944. The body of Hilfszollassistent Laber is carried out of the "Hoßfeld-Haus" through the main entrance. © *Kärntner Landesarchiv*

Kranjska Gora (Slovenia), current Borovška cesta nr. 27, November 6, 1944. Zollinspektor Guanin, BZKom (G) Kronau, pays homage to the body of Hilfszollassistent Laber outside the "Hoßfeld-Haus." © *Kärntner Landesarchiv*

Kranjska Gora (Slovenia), current Borovška cesta nr. 27, November 6, 1944. Rifle salutes in honor of Hilfszollassistent Laber outside the "Hoßfeld-Haus." © *Kärntner Landesarchiv*

November 9, 1944: A patrol of the Zollgrenzschutz clashes with five partisans near the Wurzenpass/Korensko sedlo (Alpine pass between Kreis Villach and Kreis Radmannsdorf). One partisan is killed, while two others are wounded and captured.[51]

November 11, 1944: Units subordinated to the BefSt des Zollgrenzschutzes Villach take part in a vast antipartisan operation in the area between Bohinjska Bistrica, Bled, and Mojstrana (Kreis Radmannsdorf). In this context, border guards possibly belonging to the Jagdkommando des Zollgrenzschutzes Meistern ambush a partisan unit resting for the night at some Alpine huts on the Karavanke mountains, between Dovje and the Dovška Planina, northeast of Mojstrana. Six partisans are killed in the ambush. On the same day in the Bohinj basin, German units take part in an operation under the direction of Major der Schutzpolizei Willi Hannebauer

Area of Mala Pišnica–Planica (Kranjska Gora, Slovenia), 1944–45. Border guards subordinated to the BZKom (G) Kronau pose at an unidentified plateau among the localities of Mala Pišnica and Planica during a *Grosseinsatz*. In the background, Mount Visoka Ponca, on which ran the Reichsgrenze; the snow-covered slope, no longer existing, overlooked the current ski complex of the "Planica Nordic Center." © *Kärntner Landesarchiv*

apparently commander both of the Diensthundabteilung der Waffen-SS "Südost" and of the Sicherungsabschnitt VII (Bled). Subordinated to him during the operation is a dog unit referred to as "SS-Hundestaffel Veldes" (or members of the Diensthundabteilung der Waffen-SS "Südost," which was stationed in Bled), border guards subordinated to the BZKom (G) Wocheiner-Feistritz, and policemen of the Gendarmerieposten Wocheiner-Feistritz, Neuming and Göriach. In particular, border guards of the GASt Wocheiner-Feistritz-West are engaged in fighting with partisan units in the area of Bohinjska Češnjica; during this action, in the locality of Planina Uskovnica, a partisan is killed, some huts considered partisan shelters are set on fire, and a local Slovenian serving in the Luftwaffe is mistakenly killed and his house set on fire. Furthermore, another partisan is killed in the area of Sv. Janez. Apparently, also in this context and in retaliation for an attack against the SS-Erholungsheim (sanatorium of the SS), stationed at the Hotel "Erika" near Kranjska Gora, which took place on October 25, border guards subordinated to the BZKom (G) Kronau, including Oberzollsekretär Pfister, seem to have taken part in a vast antipartisan operation (*Grosseinsatz*) in the locality of Mala Pišnica, a secondary valley between Kranjska Gora and the border crossing of Prelaz Vršič (Kreis Radmannsdorf). The operation was probably organized on the basis of information obtained from a partisan captured on November 2 near the SS-Erholungsheim, who indicated the presence of a partisan camp in the area south of Kranjska Gora. The action also seems to affect the massif of the Vitranc, a mountainous area that separates the Mala Pišnica from the Planica. Nothing is known about the conduct of the operation, with the exception of the capture of a partisan, after a firefight, by the border guards of Oberzollsekretär Pfister.[52]

Area of Mala Pišnica (Kranjska Gora, Slovenia), 1944–45. Zollsekretär Pfister (*on the right*) during a *Grosseinsatz*; the young man in civilian clothes visible in both photos is a captured partisan. © *Kärntner Landesarchiv*

November 14, 1944: Zollsekretär Exner, *Postenführer* of GASt Wocheiner-Feistritz-Süd, is killed in action against the partisans, in unclear circumstances. The place of his death, generically referred to as "Feistritz/Oberkrain," is probably to be identified with the village of Bistrica, between Črnomelj and Kočevje (Provinz Laibach). In fact, at the time of his killing, Exner was posted for a training course at the Bandenkampfschule Sittich, based in Stična (Provinz Laibach). Between November 14 and 15, members of the Bandenkampfschule Sittich apparently take part in an antipartisan operation in the locality of Miklarji, a few hundred meters away from Bistrica. On November 14, a German policeman posted to the Bandenkampfschule Sittich is reported fallen in an unknown location. On November 15, the 10. Kompanie of the SS-Polizei-Regiment 14 suffers some losses in Nemška Loka, around 5 km west of Miklarji; apparently also during this fighting, Hilfszollassistent Paulitsch dies and one *Hilfszollassistent* from the GASt Leskoutza (HZA Krainburg) is wounded.[53] On November 14, border guards of the GASt Thörl-Maglern take part in an antipartisan action in the area of Draschitz-Hohenthurn, near Feistritz an der Gail (Kreis Villach). During a clash with the partisans, which takes place during a search of the Schnabl barns, Zollsekretär Ibler, *Postenführer* of GASt Thörl-Maglern, is killed and an *Hilfszollassistent* is wounded. Zollhundeführer and Hilfszollbetriebsassistent Josef Hauptmann with the *Zollhund* "Elsta," assigned to the post, also participate to the search. The *Zollhund* "Elsta," set out in pursuit of the partisans fleeing after the firefight, is taken under fire and reported as missing. It will return on its own to the headquarters of the GASt Thörl-Maglern the following day.[54]

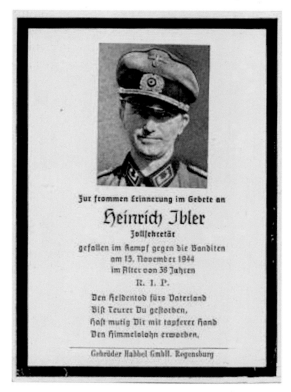

The death card of Zollsekretär Heinrich Ibler, *Postenführer* of GASt Thörl-Maglern, killed by the partisans in the area of Draschitz-Hohenthurn (Kreis Villach) on November 14, 1944. © *Goris Archive*

November 24, 1944: Border guards of the GASt Zarz and Wocheiner-Feistritz-West, under the command of the *Postenführer* of GASt Zarz, Zollsekretär Kellner, take part in an antipartisan action in the area of Davča (Kreis Krainburg). The action is set up following a report regarding the passage of a large partisan formation, coming from the area of Novaki (Provincia di Gorizia) during the previous days. Some local Volksdeutscher, enlisted as *Hilfswilliger* in the GASt Zarz, distinguish themselves due to the spirit shown during the fierce fighting. Three partisans are killed and three others are captured, while an unspecified number are wounded during this operation. Furthermore, a conspicuous number of weapons are captured. The Leiter der BefSt des Zollgrenzschutzes Villach, Zollrat Rapf, will later personally compliment Zollsekretär Kellner and the men subordinated to him during the operation for the results obtained.[55]

November 28, 1944: The Zolljagdzug Mallestig takes part in an action near Goritschach (Kreis Villach). The platoon captures two partisans and destroys three bunkers considered their shelters.[56]

Note: As recalled earlier, in late 1944–early 1945, most of the *Dienststelle* of the BefSt des Zollgrenzschutzes Villach were gradually integrated into the organizational structure of the Abteilung Zollgrenzschutz Oberkrain in Krainburg.

December 6, 1944: Members of the *Stab* of the BZKom (G) Wocheiner-Feistritz, of the GASt Wocheiner-Feistritz, along with twelve policemen of the Gendarmerie-Hochgebirgsposten Wocheiner-Feistritz, sweep the settlements of Bohinjska Češnjica, Srednja vas v Bohinju, and Stara Fužina (Kreis Radmannsdorf) in order to clear the area from the partisan presence. For this operation, all the men are apparently placed under the command of the BZKom (G) Wocheiner-Feistritz, Walter Kasischke. In the locality of Voje, north of Stara Fužina, the German column clashes with the partisans; during the firefight, which lasts about five hours, a partisan is captured and two are wounded, while six others are killed. At nightfall, during the return march, the column clashes again with the partisans near Sv. Janez.[57]

December 7, 1944: A patrol of the Zollgrenzschutz clashes with a group of six partisans approximately 7 km southwest of Faak am See (Kreis Villach); the location of the firefight, indicated as "Pkt. 1427," corresponds to the Goritschacher Alm, close to the former "Polizeigrenze" line along the Karavanke mountains. The commander of the partisan unit is killed during the fighting, while four of his men are taken prisoner. Apparently, a patrol of the Zollgrenzschutz clashes in the same area with the partisans also on December 12; during this firefight a partisan is killed.[58]

December 13, 1944: Border guards subordinated to the BZKom (G) Wocheiner-Feistritz, along with a patrol of the Gendarmerie-Hochgebirgsposten Wocheiner-Feistritz, rush to help the guards of the fortification works at the Sava bridge near Bitnje, north of Bohinjska Bistrica (Kreis Radmannsdorf), severely attacked by a partisan unit.[59]

December 18, 1944: A reconnaissance patrol, made up of twelve policemen of the Gendarmerie-Hochgebirgsposten Legenfeld and eight border guards of the GASt Meistern, intervenes in the locality of Zgornja Radovna, south of Mojstrana (Kreis Radmannsdorf) following a report about partisans looting food. Arriving in the area west of Planina Mežakla, after a brief firefight the patrol locates and destroys a partisan shelter. On the way back, along the road Mojstrana-Zgornja Radovna, the patrol falls victim to an ambush set up by the partisans positioned on the surroundings heights; after half an hour of fighting, the partisans withdraw. An *Hilfszollbetriebsassistent* is seriously wounded during the firefight.[60]

February 18, 1945: At dawn, a reconnaissance patrol coming from Bohinjska Bistrica, formed by twenty-eight border guards of the GASt Wocheiner-Feistritz-West and some *Zollhund*, falls into a partisan ambush blockade near the villages of Savica and Brod (Kreis Radmannsdorf). Due to the intensity of the fighting, some border guards are forced to ford the Sava River under strong partisan fire. After a couple of hours of fighting, the partisan unit is forced to disengage due to the arrival of German reinforcements from Bohinjska Bela. Two *Zollhund* and four border guards are killed in the firefight; they were Hilfszollassistent Ferstl, Lassmann, Pfeifer, and Rehe. Also wounded are apparently at least eight members of the patrol, including three *Hilfszollassistent*, who are taken to the Reserve-Lazarett Klagenfurt Ic, where they are awarded the Verwundetenabzeichen in Schwarz (Badge for First and Second Wounds). As a result of the clashes, some buildings are also set on fire, and at least one civilian is killed.[61]

March 3 and 7, 1945: The headquarters of the GASt Wocheiner-Feistritz (Kreis Radmannsdorf) is attacked by the partisans with mortar fire and *Panzerbüchsenbeschuss* (antitank rifle fire).[62]

March 10, 1945: A patrol belonging to the GASt Zarz falls into an ambush near Torka, east of Zgornje Danje, on the southern slopes of the Ratitovec massif (Kreis Krainburg). The border guards manage to repel the harsh attack, but one *Hilfszollassistent* belonging to the post is wounded and hospitalized at the Reserve-Lazarett Klagenfurt Ic, where he is awarded the Verwundetenabzeichen in Schwarz. On the same day, perhaps in the same context, border guards of the GASt Petersberg clash with the partisans in a location indicated as "Meidlitschbauer," probably identified with the settlement of Majdelc in the locality of Podporezen (Kreis Krainburg), close to the Reichsgrenze.[63]

March 17, 1945: The partisans try, unsuccessfully, to force the GASt Zarz (Kreis Krainburg) to surrender.[64]

March 20–April 5, 1945: Units subordinated to the BZKom (G) Wocheiner-Feistritz are widely employed in the context of the Unternehmen Frühlingsanfang, a large antipartisan operation (*Grosseinsatz*) held astride the Reichsgrenze in the area of Cerkno (Provincia di Gorizia). The action is organized in collaboration between the two Führungsstab für Bandenbekämpfung of Rösener and Globocnik. In this context, border guards subordinated to the BZKom (G) Wocheiner-Feistritz are mainly engaged in the second line as rearguard for the units of the SS-Polizei-Regiment 13. The latter, coming from the sector of Bohinjska Bistrica-Ratitovec massif (between Kreis Krainburg and Radmannsdorf), starting on March 19–20, gradually sweep the area toward the southwest. Around March 22, the units of SS-Polizei-Regiment 13 move toward Mount Porezen (Provincia di Gorizia) in an attempt to encircle the partisan formations concentrated in the area of Cerkno. In this context, on March 24–25, policemen of SS-Polizei-Regiment 13 are reported to have shot about 150 partisans captured during the operation in the area between the Davča (Kreis Krainburg) and the village of Jesenica (Provincia di Gorizia); given the losses suffered by SS-Polizei-Regiment 13 during the same days in Jesenica and on Mount Porezen, it is reasonable to assume that the shooting of the prisoners was intended as retaliation.

The main task entrusted to the Zollgrenzschutz at this stage is to clean up the area from small partisan groups that start flowing into the Bohinj basin to escape the ongoing operations, through a widespread setup of *Lauerstellung* (ambush blockades). At the same time, border guard patrols are deployed within the same area for intercepting and rounding up retreating or disengaging partisan units. The strategy used in this context is essentially that of keeping the partisan groups on the move through repeated small roundups conducted by the patrols, directing them into the *Lauerstellung* "nets," where they will be captured or annihilated. For the concentration of the partisans and stragglers captured in this context, a special collection camp is set up in Podbrdo (Provincia di Gorizia), referred to as Auffanglager Piedicolle.

Thanks to detailed information of German origin, it was possible to reconstruct the daily activity of the units of the Zollgrenzschutz during the operation; in the following descriptions are all the currently available data.

On March 20, border guards of the GASt Petersberg and Zarz capture in the area of Sorica (Kreis Krainburg) fifteen partisans who had previously managed to slip unscathed through the guarded perimeter of the ongoing operation.

On March 24, border guards of the GASt Petersberg catch two partisans in Petrovo Brdo (Provincia di Gorizia).

On March 25, border guards of the GASt Petersberg capture a wounded partisan at the "Wolfbauer" farm, near Petrovo Brdo (Provincia di Gorizia). On the same day, three partisan stragglers surrender at the headquarters of the GASt Petersberg in order to be enlisted as *Hilfswilliger*; two others are captured, after a brief firefight, apparently at the crossroads of Štadler, west of Sorica (Kreis Krainburg).

On March 26, a patrol of the GASt Zarz wounds and captures a partisan hiding in a cabin located on Mount Možic (Provincia di Gorizia); another stranded partisan is captured during the same action. On the same day, on the basis of information collected by the GASt Zarz, about sixty border guards subordinated to the BZKom (G) Wocheiner-Feistritz set up, near Ravne v Bohinju (Kreis Radmannsdorf), an ambush blockade to intercept a partisan unit fleeing from Mount Porezen (Provincia di Gorizia). However, in the hours preceding the ambush, the partisan unit manages to regroup unscathed in the Bohinj basin; after attacking an unidentified post of the Zollgrenzschutz around Bohinjska Bistrica and searching the area for food, in the following days the partisan unit takes refuge on Mount Rudnica, near the village of Brod (Kreis Radmannsdorf).

On March 27, a local Volksdeutscher, forcibly enlisted by the partisans, manages to flee and reaches the headquarters of the GASt Zarz (Kreis Krainburg); he is, however, detained at the Auffanglager Piedicolle. On the same day, border guards of the GASt Petersberg arrest three partisans, two Italians, and one Frenchman at the "Wolfbauer" farm in Petrovo Brdo (Provincia di Gorizia), who had been forcibly enlisted in the area of Cerkno; they are later sent to the KdS Veldes headquarters.

On March 30, border guards of the GASt Petersberg set up an ambush blockade in the locality of "Blechschneider" (unidentified), while a patrol of the same post sweeps the area toward Podbrdo (Provincia di Gorizia).

On March 31, the GASt Wocheiner-Feistritz sets up an ambush blockade around Nemški Rovt (Kreis Radmannsdorf) while a patrol of the same post sweeps the area from Ravne v Bohinju toward the locality of "Granica" (unidentified, perhaps the former Graničarji facility of Rovti near the current "Mencingerjeva Koča" hut, Kreis Radmannsdorf).

On April 1, two patrols of the GASt Wocheiner-Feistritz are again in action from Ravne v Bohinju toward the localities of "Granica" and Nemški Rovt (Kreis Radmannsdorf); at the same time, the GASt Wocheiner-Feistritz-West sets up an ambush blockade near the railway bridge of Bitnje (Kreis Radmannsdorf), and an *Ortsstreife* (urban patrol) and a second ambush blockade in the area of the "Menzinger" farm (probably identified with the current "Mencingerjeva Koča" hut)—*Forstamt* (forestry office). On the same day, the GASt Petersberg sets up two ambush blockades, one on the road bend toward Podbrdo (Provincia di Gorizia) and one near Trojar (Kreis Krainburg); the post also sends a roundup patrol in the area of the border crossing of Rovtar and Podhočar, in the locality of Podporezen (Kreis Krainburg). Also on April 1, the GASt Zarz sends a sweep patrol into the area between Sorica-Spodnje Danje-Roktar (Kreis Krainburg).

On April 2, the GASt Wocheiner-Feistritz sends a sweep patrol in the area between Ravne v Bohinju and a locality indicated as "Miggitshütte gegen Strümpe" (unidentified; apparently one of the huts located in Planina Strmne near Nemški Rovt) and sets up a sweep patrol and an ambush blockade in the area south of the Austro-Hungarian military cemetery of Bohinjska Bistrica (Kreis Radmannsdorf). At the same time, the GASt Wocheiner-Feistritz-West sets up, at the railway bridge of Bitnje, an ambush blockade toward the village of Brod (Kreis Radmannsdorf). The GASt Petersberg sets up two ambush blockades, one in Rovtar in the locality of Podporezen (Kreis Krainburg) and the other one on the road bend toward Podbrdo (Provincia di Gorizia), employing at the same time a sweep patrol within this area. The GASt Zarz sends two patrols in the area of Podrošt (Kreis Krainburg), one toward the settlement of Spodnje Danje and the other one through the Selška Sora valley; during the patrolling, two partisan stragglers are captured.

On April 3, border guards of the GASt Wocheiner-Feistritz patrol the area between Ravne v Bohinju and Nemški Rovt while personnel of the GASt Wocheiner-Feistritz-West set up an ambush blockade at the sawmills located west of Bohinjska Bistrica (Kreis Radmannsdorf). On the same day, a patrol of the GASt Petersberg sweeps the area of Mount Lajnar, north of Petrovo Brdo, and contextually sets up an ambush blockade near the Italian bunkers located on Mount Možic (Provincia di Gorizia). Border guards of the GASt Zarz apparently set up an ambush blockade between the settlement of Rotkar and the crossroads of Štadler (Kreis Krainburg) and sweep the forest that stretches across the Reichsgrenze between the villages of Sorica and Petrovo Brdo (between Kreis Krainburg and Provincia di Gorizia).

On April 4, a two-phase reconnaissance action is organized in order to probe the consistency of the partisan unit, estimated at approximately eight hundred men, that gathered at the end of March in some bunkers on Mount Rudnica, near the village of Brod (Kreis Radmannsdorf). In the action, apparently directed by the BZKom (G) Wocheiner-Feistritz, two *Kampfgruppe* (battle groups) take part. The first one, named Kampfgruppe Herppich (from the name of the *Abteilungsführer* in Petersberg, Zollinspektor Karl Herppich, who at that date also seems to be acting as deputy of the BZKom (G) Wocheiner-Feistritz), is made up of border guards subordinated to the BZKom (G) Wocheiner-Feistritz, two *Sturmzug* (assault platoons) of the Landesschützen-Bataillon 927, policemen of the Gendarmerieposten Wocheiner-Feistritz, an artillery unit based in Bohinjska Bela (likely belonging to the Gebirgs-Nebelwerfer-Lehr-und Ausbildungs-Batterie 6), and members of a unit indicated as "Hundesstaffel Veldes" (certainly belonging to the Diensthundabteilung der Waffen-SS "Südost"), for a total of 140 men. The second battle group, named Kampfgruppe Broszeit (from the name of the *Postenführer* of GASt Wocheiner-Feistritz-West, Zollsekretär Broszeit), is formed by border guards subordinated to the BZKom (G) Wocheiner-Feistritz, two *Sturmzug* of the Landesschützen-Bataillon 927, and members of the Gendarmerieposten

Neuming, for a total of eighty men. The action involves, in the first phase, a pincer movement carried out by the two *Kampfgruppe*, starting from Bohinjska Bistrica and implemented in the direction of the village of Laški Rovt. At dawn of April 4, Kampfgruppe Herppich receives the order to patrol the area of the Dobrava up to the inhabited area of Polje and to stop in the latter location; Kampfgruppe Broszeit, starting out one hour later, is ordered to march from Bohinjska Bistrica up to the village of Brod, where it must stop near the bridge over the Sava. During this first phase, Kampfgruppe Herppich also has the task of sweeping the villages of Žlan, Polje, and Laški Rovt, while Kampfgruppe Broszeit those of Brod, Savica, and Kamnje. At 6:30 a.m., when the second phase of the operation starts, the two *Kampfgruppe* receive the order to regroup in the area west of Laški Rovt, under the cover ensured by thirty men of the "Flak Assling" (probably belonging to the le. Flak-Ausbildungs-Abteilung 699), controlling the bridge over the Sava near Brod. It has not been possible to find detailed data about the progress and results of the operation; however, it seems that the German units were widely involved in harsh clashes with the partisans along the route Savica–Kamnje–Laški–Rovt–Sv. Janez.

Also on April 4, border guards of the GASt Petersberg sweep the settlements of Rovtar and Podhočar in the locality of Podporezen, then march in the direction of the village of Pri Zagi (Kreis Krainburg). On the same day, the GASt Zarz sets up two ambush blockades in the villages of Rotkar and Sorica and at the same time sends sweep patrols into the area between Sorica and Torka (Kreis Krainburg), which capture a partisan straggler in the latter location.

On April 5, the GASt Wocheiner-Feistritz sets up an ambush blockade and at the same time conducts a sweep operation in the area between Nemški Rovt and Ravne v Bohinju–Granica (Kreis Radmannsdorf). On the same day, border guards of the GASt Petersberg continue to be engaged in roundups near Rovtar and Podhočar, in the locality of Podporezen, and in the area of Pri Zagi (Kreis Krainburg). Also on April 5, the GASt Zarz sets up three ambush blockades. One is set up between the villages of Sorica and Spodnje Danje, one in the area of Rotkar, and one in the southern part of the settlement of Sorica (Kreis Krainburg); in addition, at an interval of one hour from each other, two patrols belonging to the post are sent to sweep the area of Pri Zagi (Kreis Krainburg), probably in support to the border guards of the GASt Petersberg engaged in action in the same locality.[65]

CHAPTER 10
The Last Weeks of War

By March 29, while the Unternehmen Frühlingsanfang was in full swing, the BZKom (G) Wocheiner-Feistritz informed the Abteilung Zollgrenzschutz Oberkrain in Krainburg that a considerable number of partisans, trying to escape the operations in progress in the area of Cerkno (Provincia di Gorizia), had managed to slip unscathed through the guarded perimeter of the ongoing operation and poured inside the Reich into the Bohinj basin (Kreis Radmannsdorf) and in the Davča (Kreis Krainburg). In particular it was highlighted that during the last days of April, a large partisan unit made up of 150 men was concentrated astride the Reichsgrenze in the area between Mount Možic–Mount Porezen–Davča–Novaki–Zali Log–Ratitovec massif. For this reason the BZKom (G) Wocheiner-Feistritz suggested the organization of another large-scale operation (*Grosseinsatz*) within the aforementioned area, noting that particular attention had to be paid to the reclamation of the sector of Bohinjska Bistrica (in which, as seen, on the following April 4, an antipartisan operation was actually carried out). The BZKom (G) Wocheiner-Feistritz also reported that, in mid-April, a large number of corpses of partisans killed during the Unternehmen Frühlingsanfang were still scattered throughout the area of the Davča; they were certainly, at least in part, the partisans shot by members of SS-Polizei-Regiment 13 on March 24–25. So, although it is not entirely clear whether or not in the context of a further large operation, even after the conclusion of the Unternehmen Frühlingsanfang, the units subordinated to the BZKom (G) Wocheiner-Feistritz continued to be widely used to intercept the partisans who had converged in the aforementioned areas during the preceding weeks. The information available on this last operating cycle is shown below.[1]

April 6, 1945: The villages of Bohinjska Bistrica and Nomenj (Kreis Radmannsdorf) are heavily attacked by the partisans. Probably in this context, the GASt Wocheiner-Feistritz-West sets up an ambush blockade between the rail bridge and the village of Bitnje (Kreis Radmannsdorf). On the same day, the GASt Zarz sets up an ambush blockade at the crossroads of Štadler (Kreis Krainburg), while three patrols of the post sweep the area in the directions of Petrovo Brdo, Travh-Mount Lajnar, and Zabrdo-Torka (between Kreis Krainburg and Provincia di Gorizia).

April 7, 1945: The GASt Wocheiner-Feistritz sets up an ambush blockade between Ravne v Bohinju and the locality of "Strümpe" (unidentified; probably Planina Strmne near Nemški Rovt, Kreis Radmannsdorf). The GASt Wocheiner-Feistritz-West is committed to the protection of the railway line near Lepence and in patrolling the area of the Dobrava, near Bohinjska Bistrica (Kreis Radmannsdorf). On the same day, border guards of the GASt Petersberg patrol the area between Petrovo Brdo and Podbrdo (Provincia di Gorizia), while the GASt Zarz sets up two ambush blockades near the village of Podrošt (Kreis Krainburg).

April 8, 1945: Border guards of the GASt Wocheiner-Feistritz sweep the area of Nemški Rovt, while those of the GASt Wocheiner-Feistritz-West are still busy patrolling the area of the Dobrava (Kreis Radmannsdorf). The GASt Petersberg sets up an ambush blockade at the road bend toward Podbrdo and sweeps the settlement of Robar (Provincia di Gorizia). On the same day, border guards of the GASt Zarz sweep the area of Ravne, near Torka, and set up an ambush blockade on Mount Tonderškofel (Kreis Krainburg).

April 9, 1945: Border guards of the GASt Wocheiner-Feistritz-West are employed at the bridge of Bitnje (Kreis Radmannsdorf) to set up an ambush blockade and protect the railway line. Two patrols belonging to the GASt Petersberg and Zarz jointly sweep the area of the Davča (Kreis Krainburg), killing three partisans and capturing two others.

April 10, 1945: Border guards of the GASt Zarz, apparently grouped into two separate patrols, sweep the area toward the villages of Petrovo Brdo (Provincia di Gorizia) and Torka (Kreis Krainburg), killing two partisans in the latter location.

April 11, 1945: Border guards of the GASt Wocheiner-Feistritz-West set up an ambush blockade in the area of the Dobrava, near Bohinjska Bistrica, while a patrol of the GASt Wocheiner-Feistritz sweeps the area of Ravne v Bohinju (Kreis Radmannsdorf). The GASt Petersberg sets up an ambush blockade at the road bend toward Podbrdo (Provincia di Gorizia), while the GASt Zarz sends a patrol to sweep the area in the direction of Spodnje Danje and sets up an ambush blockade near the villages of Rotkar and Podrošt (Kreis Krainburg).

April 12, 1945: Border guards of the GASt Wocheiner-Feistritz-West are employed for the protection of the railway near Lepence (Kreis Radmannsdorf). A patrol of the GASt Zarz sweeps the area of Mount Možic (Provincia di Gorizia) and later toward Ravne v Bohinju (Kreis Radmannsdorf). During April 11–12, border guards of the GASt Petersberg set up an ambush blockade in "Meidlitschbauer," probably identified with the settlement of Majdelc, located close to the Reichsgrenze in the locality of Podporezen (Kreis Krainburg), later sweeping Mount Porezen and Mount Hoč (Provincia di Gorizia).

As a last note to this final cycle of operations, according to sources of the BZKom (G) Wocheiner-Feistritz, the activity of the GASt Petersberg and Zarz alone had led to the killing of five partisans and the capture of another fourteen, while twenty-three local *Freiwilliger*, captured and forcibly impressed by the partisans, had been freed and reincorporated in their former units.

Nothing is known about the border guard units originally subordinated to the HZA Villach / BefSt des Zollgrenzschutzes Villach during the last days of the war, with one exception: on the night between May 4 and 5, partisan elements that attack the fortified headquarters of the BZKom (G) Kronau and of the ZASt (G) Kronau are quickly pushed back by the border guards. The following morning, having learned of the arrival of large partisan formations in Kranjska Gora, the border guards based in the village join a long column of refugees headed to the Kreis Villach, where they end their service in British captivity. The same fate probably befell a good part of the members of the Abteilung Zollgrenzschutz Oberkrain in Krainburg, who survived the last days of war in the Kreis Radmannsdorf, Kreis Krainburg, and Provincia di Gorizia.[2]

The Reichsfinanzverwaltung identification badges of two members of the Zollgrenzschutz serving in Bohinjska Bistrica (Wocheiner-Feistritz) and Rateče-Planica (Ratschach-Matten). © *Kärntner Landesarchiv*

APPENDIXES

APPENDIX I
Map of the Hauptzollamt Villach's Dienststelle Locations

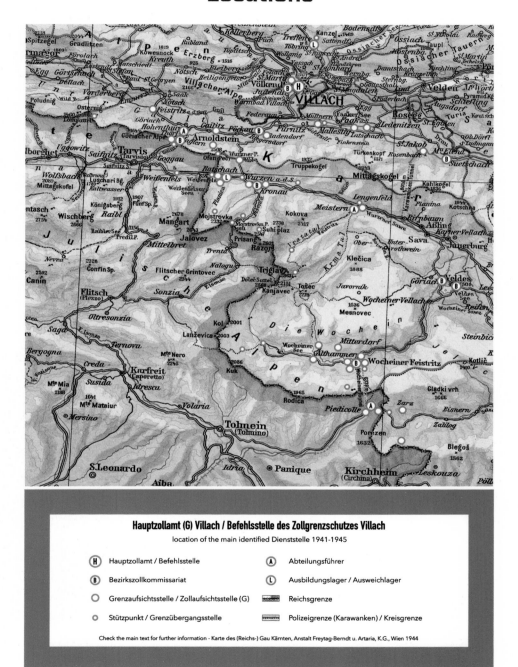

Hauptzollamt (G) Villach / Befehlsstelle des Zollgrenzschutzes Villach

location of the main identified Dienststelle 1941-1945

(H) Hauptzollamt / Befehlsstelle

(B) Bezirkszollkommissariat

O Grenzaufsichtsstelle / Zollaufsichtsstelle (G)

o Stützpunkt / Grenzübergangsstelle

(A) Abteilungsführer

(L) Ausbildungslager / Ausweichlager

▬ Reichsgrenze

▬ Polizeigrenze (Karawanken) / Kreisgrenze

Check the main text for further information - Karte des (Reichs-) Gau Kärnten, Anstalt Freytag-Berndt u. Artaria, K.G., Wien 1944

APPENDIX II
Chart of the Hauptzollamt Villach's Organizational Structure 1941–1945

Oberfinanzpräsidium (G) Graz
- Abteilung Zoll
- Grenzreferat Graz

Hauptzollamt (G) Villach

BZKom (G) Arnoldstein (1939–1943)
- Ausbildungslager
- GÜSt Coccau / Thörl
- GÜSt Fusine / Rateče

- GASt / ZASt (G) Arnoldstein
- GASt Kronau
- ZASt (G) Kronau
- ZASt (G) Mallestig
- GASt Ratschach-Matten °
  - Stp. Richter-Haus *
  - Stp. Strametz-Haus
- ZASt (G) Ratschach-Matten-Nord °
- GASt / ZASt (G) Ratschach-Matten-Süd
- ZASt (G) Riegersdorf
- ZASt (G) Thörl-Maglern
- GASt Feistritz an der Gail *

BZKom (G) Kronau (1943–1945)
- GÜSt Coccau / Thörl
- GÜSt Fusine / Rateče
- Stp. Fusine in Valromana *

- GASt Arnoldstein
- GASt Kronau
  - Stp. Mojstrovkapass
- ZASt (G) Kronau
  - Stp. Mojstrovkapass *
  - Stp. Wald *
  - Stp. Wurzen *
- GASt Ratschach-Matten
  - Stp. Richter-Haus
  - Stp. Strametz-Haus
- GASt Wurzenpass
- **Abteilungsführer in Meistern ***
  - JaKo Meistern
  - Zollhunde-Übungslager
- GASt Meistern
  - Stp. Aljaž-Haus *
- **Abteilungsführer in Thörl-Maglern ***
  - Ausweichlager
  - Stp. Mallestig
- GASt Feistritz an der Gail
- GASt / ZASt (G) Thörl-Maglern

BZKom (G) Thörl-Maglern (1944–1945)
- Ausweichlager
- GÜSt Coccau / Thörl
- Stp. Mallestig

- GASt / ZASt (G) Feistritz an der Gail
  - Stp. Feistritzer Alm
- GASt Seltschach °
- GASt Thörl-Maglern °

BZKom (G) St. Jakob im Rosental (1939–1941)
- ZASt (G) Rosenbach
- ZASt (G) Woroutz
- ZASt (G) Latschach *

// 106 \\

Note: in late 1944 the Hauptzollamt (G) Villach changed its name to Befehlsstelle des Zollgrenzschutzes Villach

BZKom = Bezirkszollkommissariat; GASt = Grenzaufsichtsstelle; GÜSt = Grenzübergangsstelle; GZSt = Grenzzollstelle; JaKo = Jagdkommando;
Stp. = Höhenstützpunkt, Stützpunkt, Talstützpunkt; ZA = Zollamt; ZASt = Zollaufsichtsstelle; (E) = Eisenbahnzollamt; (G) = (mit Grenze);
(L) = Landstraßenzollamt; (St) = (Steuer); * = hypothetical data; ° = probably the same Dienststelle, Check the main text for further information

BZKom (G) Wocheiner-Feistritz (1942–1945)	GÜSt Wocheiner-Feistritz	Stp. Berta-Hütte *	JaKo Wocheiner-Feistritz
GASt Althammer	Stp. Bogatin-Sattel *	Stp. Savica	
GASt / ZASt (G) Mitterdorf in Wochein			
GASt / ZASt (G) St. Johann am Wocheinersee °	Stp. Bogatin-Sattel *	Stp. Savica *	
GASt / ZASt (G) Wocheinersee °			
GASt / ZASt (G) Wocheiner-Feistritz			
GASt / ZASt (G) Wocheiner-Feistritz-Nord			
GASt Wocheiner-Feistritz-West			
GASt Wocheiner-Feistritz-Süd			
Abteilungsführer in Petersberg			
GASt / ZASt (G) Dautscha	Stp. Zollstrasse		
GASt Petersberg			
GASt Piedicolle			
GASt / ZASt (G) Zarz	Stp. Zarz-Zollstrasse		
BZKom (G) Thörl-Maglern *			

BZKom (G) Obergöriach (1941) °			
BZKom (G) Veldes (1942–1943) °			
GASt / ZASt (G) Althammer	Stp. Berroth-Hütte *	Stp. Savica *	
GASt Kronau	Stp. Mojstrovkapass	Stp. Rathke-Haus *	
GASt / ZASt (G) Meistern	Stp. Aljaž-Haus *	Stp. Kredarica-Hütte *	Stp. Meistern *
GASt / ZASt (G) Mitterdorf in Wochein			
GASt / ZASt (G) Wocheiner-Feistritz			

BZKom (St) Villach (1939–1944)
ZASt (St) Villach *

ZA (E) Arnoldstein (GZSt *)
ZA Assling
ZA (L) Ratschach-Matten (GZSt *)
ZA (E) Villach
ZA Wocheiner-Feistritz (GZSt *)
ZA Thörl-Maglern * (GZSt *)

APPENDIX III
Chart of the Hauptzollamt Villach's Facilities

List of the identified buildings used by the Zollgrenzschutz-VGAD units subordinated to the Hauptzollamt Villach 1941–1945

* = hypothetical data ; ° = probably the same building; (DAV) = building originally belonging to the Deutscher Alpenverein (German Alpine Club)

Facility in use to the HZA Villach	Dienststelle	Original facility name
10. Oktoberstrasse 11, Villach	Hauptzollamt Villach	NSDAP-Kreisleitung (Reichsarbeitsdienst)
Pestalozzistrasse 24, Villach	Hauptzollamt Villach	Unknown
Khevenhüllergasse 22, Villach	BZKom (St) Villach	Unknown
"Aljaž-Haus", later "Kugy-Haus"	Höhenstützpunkt Aljaž-Haus	"Aljažev dom" or "Aljaž-Haus" / "Aljasch-Haus" (DAV)
"Berta-Hütte" °	Höhenstützpunkt Berta-Hütte	"Orožnova koča" or "Orožen-Hütte" (DAV)
"Berroth-Hütte"	Höhenstützpunkt Berroth-Hütte	Unknown
"Dr. Rathke-Haus"	Stützpunkt Rathke-Haus (Krnica-Tal)	"Koča v Krnici" or "Kernica-Hütte" (DAV)
"Dr. Richter-Haus"	Stützpunkt Richter-Haus (Tamar)	"Planica" facility of the Graničarji
"Dr. Sperling-Haus"	Höhenstützpunkt Mojstrovkapass	"Erjavčeva koča" or "Voss-Hütte" (DAV)
"Dr. Strametz-Haus"	Höhenstützpunkt Strametz-Haus (Ofen)	Apparently built for the purpose
"Hoßfeld-Haus"	BZKom (G) Kronau and GASt Kronau	Yugoslav Forestry Office
"Jungk-Haus"	Höhenstützpunkt Mojstrovkapass	"Klin" facility of the Graničarji
"Kärntner-Haus" *	Höhenstützpunkt Bogatin-Sattel *	"Koča pod Bogatinom" or "Bogatin-Hütte" (DAV) *
"Komna-Haus" *	Höhenstützpunkt Bogatin-Sattel *	"Dom na Komni" or "Komna-Haus" (DAV) *
"Kredarica-Hütte"	Höhenstützpunkt Kredarica-Hütte	"Triglavski dom" (DAV)
"Rindler-Hütte" °	Zollgrenzschutz-Höhenstützpunkt (?)	"Orožen-Schutzhütte" (DAV)
Gauschule Wald der NSDAP	Stützpunkt Wald	Hotel "Coop"
Nr. 1, Petersberg	GASt Petersberg	"sottotenente Ennio Poggiolini" barracks of the Guardia di Finanza
Nr. 1, Ober-Zarz	GASt Zarz	Parish of Zgornja Sorica
Nr. 2, Unter-Zarz	GASt Zarz	Schools of Spodnja Sorica
Nr. 14, Althammer	GASt Althammer	Unknown
Nr. 39, St. Johann am Wocheinersee	GASt St. Johann am Wocheinersee	Hotel "Sv. Janez" *
Nr. 88, Wocheiner-Feistritz	GASt Wocheiner-Feistritz-West	Unknown
Nr. 143, Wocheiner-Feistritz	BZKom (G) Wocheiner-Feistritz	Yugoslav railway Customs office
Nr. 177, Wocheiner-Feistritz	GASt Wocheiner-Feistritz	"Finančna kontrola" main barracks of the Graničarji *
Unknown	GASt Ratschach-Matten-Süd *	Yugoslav railway Customs office *
Unknown	GASt Wocheiner-Feistritz-Süd	"Rovti" facility of the Graničarji *
Unknown	Höhenstützpunkt Feistritzer Alm	Unknown
Unknown	Höhenstützpunkt Mojstrovkapass	"Vršič cesta" sentry box of the Graničarji
Unknown	Höhenstützpunkt Mojstrovkapass	"Vršič vrh" facility of the Graničarji
Unknown	Höhenstützpunkt Mojstrovkapass	"Moistrocca" summer detachment of the Guardia di Finanza
Unknown	Jagdkommando Wocheiner-Feistritz	Schools of Bohinjska Bistrica *
Unknown	Stützpunkt Savica	Facility of the Graničarji *
Unknown	Stützpunkt Zollstrasse (Zarz / Dautscha)	"Petrovo Brdo" facility of the Graničarji *
Unknown	ZASt (G) Kronau	Private residence *
Unknown	Unknown	Hotel "Markež"

Note for the reader: on the basis of agreements entered into with the Reichsfinanzministerium, during the war the monitoring of the "Schutzhütte" (alpine shelters) of the Deutscher Alpenverein located near the Reichsgrenze was taken over by the Zollgrenzschutz, which installed its outposts in some of these buildings. In August 1941 the Chef der Zivilverwaltung in den besetzten Gebieten Kärntens und Krains agreed for the "Schutzhütte" located in the Oberkrain to be integrated into the structure of the Deutscher Alpenverein: ÖNB, *Der Gebirgsfreund*, Jahrg. 52, Fl. 5, 08.1941, pg. 18 and *Allgemeine Schutzhütten-Zeitung*, Jahrg. 14, Fl. 12, 12.1942, pg. 5. The names and positions of the Graničarji facilities used in this chart originate from the project www.rapalskameja.si/zemljevid/

Current facility name	Current facility address
Private residence	10. Oktoberstrasse 11, Villach, Austria
Probably no longer existing	Area of the "Opel" car dealer, Pestalozzistrasse 33, Villach, Austria
Probably no longer existing	Area of Khevenhüllergasse, Villach, Austria
"Aljažev dom v Vratih"	Triglavska cesta 89, Vrata, Mojstrana, Slovenia
"Orožnova koča na planini Za Liscem pod Črno prstjo"	Ravne v Bohinju, Bohinjska Bistrica, Slovenia
Unknown	Area of Ukanc *, Bohinjska Bistrica, Slovenia
"Koča v Krnici" or "Dom Krnica"	Vršiška cesta 82, Krnica, Kranjska Gora, Slovenia
Private residence	Tamar, Rateče 168, Rateče-Planica, Slovenia
"Erjavčeva koča na Vršiču"	Vršiška cesta 90, Kranjska Gora, Slovenia
Probably no longer existing	Adjacent to the "Planinsko Društvo Peč 1509" hut, Rateče-Planica, Slovenia
Apartment "House Berghi I"	Borovška cesta 27, Kranjska Gora, Slovenia
"Mihov dom na Vršiču"	Vršiška cesta 83, Kranjska Gora, Slovenia
"Koča pod Bogatinom" *	Ukanc 148, Bohinjska Bistrica, Slovenia *
"Dom na Komni"	Ukanc 147, Bohinjska Bistrica, Slovenia
"Triglavski dom na Kredarici"	Mount Triglav, Mojstrana, Slovenia
"Orožnova koča na planini Za Liscem pod Črno prstjo" *	Ravne v Bohinju, Bohinjska Bistrica, Slovenia
Probably no longer existing	Gozd Martuljek, Slovenia
"Dom upokojencev Podbrdo"	Petrovo Brdo 7, Podbrdo, Slovenia
Unknown	Sorica, Slovenia
Unknown	Sorica, Slovenia
Unknown	Stara Fužina, Slovenia
Probably no longer existing	Area of the Snack Bar "Pod Brezo" *, Ribčev Laz 55, Bohinjsko jezero, Slovenia
Unknown	Bohinjska Bistrica, Slovenia
Železniška postaja	Triglavska cesta 1, Bohinjska Bistrica, Slovenia
Probably no longer existing	Area of Triglavska cesta 30 *, Bohinjska Bistrica, Slovenia
Probably no longer existing	Area of the house nr. 161 *, Rateče-Planica, Slovenia
Unknown	Ravne v Bohinju *, Bohinjska Bistrica, Slovenia
Unknown	Feistritz an der Gail 111, Feistritz an der Gail, Austria
Probably no longer existing	Prelaz Vršič, Kranjska Gora, Slovenia
"Poštarski dom na Vršiču"	Vršiška cesta 92, Kranjska Gora, Slovenia
"Tičarjev dom"	Trenta 85, Soča, Slovenia
Unknown	Area of Ajdovska cesta 20-24 *, Bohinjska Bistrica, Slovenia
"Koča pri Savici" *	Ukanc 103 *, Bohinjska Bistrica, Slovenia
"Carinamica" *	Podporezen 2 *, Petrovo Brdo, Slovenia
Private residence	Borovška cesta 7, Kranjska Gora, Slovenia
Gostilna "Črna prst"	Triglavska cesta 7, Bohinjska Bistrica, Slovenia

Chart of the Hauptzollamt Villach's Vehicles

List of the identified vehicles used by the Zollgrenzschutz-VGAD units subordinated to the Hauptzollamt Villach 1941–1945

HZA = Hauptzollamt; BZKom (G) = Bezirkszollkommissariat (mit Grenze); GASt = Grenzaufsichtsstelle; * = hypothetical data

Dienststelle	Vehicle	Chassis Number	
HZA Villach	Personenkraftwagen Impéria 2000 * and Steyr 1500		
BZKom (G) Kronau	Personenkraftwagen Daimler 1700		
BZKom (G) Wocheiner-Feistritz	Personenkraftwagen Steyr 1500		
BZKom (G) Kronau *	Personenkraftwagen ?		
BZKom (G) Veldes	Geländekraftwagen Tempo G 1200	1263898 *	
BZKom (G) Kronau	Geländekraftwagen Tempo G 1200	1263898 *	
GASt Piedicolle *	Geländekraftwagen Tempo G 1200	1263906	
HZA Villach	Geländekraftwagen Tempo G 1200	1263904, 1263908, 1263910	
BZKom (G) Wocheiner-Feistritz	Geländekraftwagen Tempo G 1200	1264010	
BZKom (G) Thörl-Maglern	Kraftrad BMW 740		
BZKom (G) Wocheiner-Feistritz	Kraftrad BMW 740		
BZKom (G) Kronau	Kraftrad BMW 740		
BZKom (G) Kronau *	Kraftrad NSU 600 *		
Abteilungsführer Meistern *	Kraftrad DKW 500	286921	
BZKom (G) Wocheiner-Feistritz *	Kraftrad DKW 500	430758	
GASt Wocheinersee *	Kraftrad DKW 500	433979	

Information taken from: Author's archive; BA, R2/9709, OFPräs Graz, *Tempo-Geländekraftwagen*, 16.07.1942 and no heading, *Nachweisung 2 über reichseigene Personenkraftwagen u. reichseigene Krafträder*, no date; ibid., R 2/9862, no heading, *Nachweisung 3 über beamteneigene Personenkraftwagen und Krafträder*, no date; KLA, AT-KLA 128-F-H 61, *An "Grünen Grenzen" - Denkwürdigkeiten aus der Dienstzeit im Zollgrenzschutz von Karl Pfister.*

License plate	Insignia	Time-frame	Entrusted to
		late 1944	Zollrat Rapf
		late 1944	Zollinspektor Guanin
		late 1944	BZKom (G) Kasischke
St-2783		mid 1944	Oberzollinspektor Kellerer *
		mid 1942	BZKom (G) Frischmann *
K-25014	"ZOLL"	mid 1943	Zollinspektor Guanin
		late 1944	
		late 1944	
		late 1944	
		late 1944	Beamte z.b.V. * Zollsekretär Zigoutz
		late 1944	Beamte z.b.V. Oberzollsekretär Gröschel
St-8220	Airbomb	late 1944	Beamte z.b.V. Zollsekretär Pfister
K-400021		1943-1944	
62 *		late 1944	
St-8259 *		late 1944	
St-8251 *		late 1944	

APPENDIX V
Chart of the Organizational Structure of the Zollgrenzschutz-VGAD under the Oberfinanzpräsidium Graz in the Reichsgau Kärnten and Steiermark and Occupied Territories, late 1939–late 1944

BefSt = Befehlsstelle; * = hypothetical data

1939–1940	early 1941	late 1941
Hauptzollamt (G) Graz	Hauptzollamt (G) Graz	Hauptzollamt (G) Fürstenfeld
Hauptzollamt (G) Graz-Grenze	Hauptzollamt (G) Fürstenfeld	Hauptzollamt (G) Lienz
Hauptzollamt (G) Fürstenfeld	Hauptzollamt (G) Lienz	Hauptzollamt (G) Klagenfurt
Hauptzollamt (G) Leoben	Hauptzollamt (G) Klagenfurt	Hauptzollamt (G) Villach
Hauptzollamt (G) Lienz	Hauptzollamt (G) Villach	BefSt d. Zollgrenzschutzes Cilli
Hauptzollamt (G) Klagenfurt		BefSt d. Zollgrenzschutzes Krainburg
Hauptzollamt (G) Villach		BefSt d. Zollgrenzschutzes Marburg/Drau

BefSt = Befehlsstelle; * = hypothetical data

1942	late 1943–mid 1944	late 1944
Hauptzollamt (G) Fürstenfeld	Hauptzollamt (G) Fürstenfeld	BefSt d. Zollgrenzschutzes Fürstenfeld
Hauptzollamt (G) Lienz	Hauptzollamt (G) Lienz	BefSt d. Zollgrenzschutzes Lienz
Hauptzollamt (G) Klagenfurt	Hauptzollamt (G) Klagenfurt *	BefSt d. Zollgrenzschutzes Villach
Hauptzollamt (G) Villach	Hauptzollamt (G) Villach	BefSt d. Zollgrenzschutzes Cilli
Hauptzollamt (G) Cilli	Hauptzollamt (G) Cilli	BefSt d. Zollgrenzschutzes Krainburg
Hauptzollamt (G) Krainburg	Hauptzollamt (G) Krainburg	BefSt d. Zollgrenzschutzes Marburg/Drau
Hauptzollamt (G) Marburg/Drau	Hauptzollamt (G) Marburg/Drau	BefSt d. Zollgrenzschutzes Arch *
	BefSt d. Zollgrenzschutzes Laibach (OZAK)	

APPENDIX VI
Chart of the Organizational Structure of the Zollgrenzschutz-VGAD under the Befehlshaber der Sicherheitspolizei und des SD Salzburg in the Reichsgau Kärnten and Steiermark and Occupied Territories, late 1944–early 1945

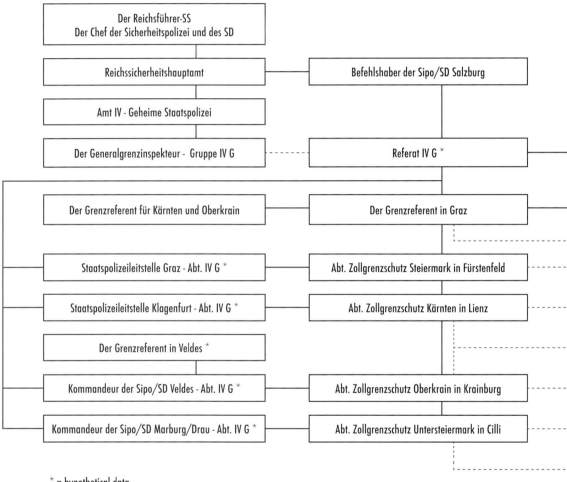

* = hypothetical data
Abt. = Abteilung
BefSt = Befehlsstelle

Der Grenzreferent in Salzburg *

Der Grenzreferent für Steiermark und Untersteiermark

BefSt d. Zollgrenzschutzes Fürstenfeld *

BefSt d. Zollgrenzschutzes Lienz

BefSt d. Zollgrenzschutzes Villach

BefSt d. Zollgrenzschutzes Krainburg

BefSt d. Zollgrenzschutzes Cilli

BefSt d. Zollgrenzschutzes Marburg/Drau *

BefSt d. Zollgrenzschutzes Arch *

List of the *Zoll* Ranks

Zoll-Dienstgrade, 1937–1945

Reichsminister der Finanzen

Staatssekretär

Generalinspekteur des Zollgrenzschutzes / Ministerialdirektor

Oberfinanzpräsident

Finanzpräsident Zoll / Ministerialrat

Oberregierungsrat

Oberzollrat/Regierungsrat

Zollrat

Zollfinanzrat

Zollamtmann

Oberzollinspektor / Regierungsassessor / Bezirkszollkommissar

Zollinspektor

außerplanmäßiger Zollinspektor

Oberzollsekretär

Zollsekretär / Hilfszollsekretär

Zollassistent/Hilfszollassistent

außerplanmäßiger Zollassistent

Zollbetriebsassitent / Hilfszollbetriebsassistent

Zolloberwachtmeister

Zollwachtmeister

Finanzanwärter Zoll

Zollanwärter

Zollgrenzangestellter

APPENDIX VIII
Place-Names in German, Italian, and Slovenian

Most of the localities and toponyms cited in this study are currently found in Austria and Slovenia. In order to facilitate their identification, it was decided to use in the text their current name. The German toponymy for the Oberkrain varied significantly due to the use of several versions—more or less obsolete—of the same toponym. For the current study, the versions used were taken from ARS, SI AS 2173, t.e. 49; Gendarmeriekreis Radmannsdorf, *Verzeichnis*, 04.07.1941; W. Rachle, *Oberkrainer Gemeindegeschäftkalendar für das Rechungsjahr* 1944 (Assling–Oberkrain, Slovenia: Buchdruckerei A. Blaschei, 1943); and *Gemeinde-und Ortschaftsverzeichnis der an den Reichsgau Kärnten angegliederten befreiten Gebiete Oberkrains und Unterkärntens* (Vienna: Verlag der Publikationsstelle Wien, 1942).

Ge.: = German, It.: = Italian, Sl.: = Slovenian, Cr.: = Croatian
(h) = Alpine hut, (p) = Alpine pass, (v) = valley

Aljažev dom v Vratih (Ge.: Aljaž-Haus), locality of Vrata near Mojstrana, Slovenia (h)
Alt-Finkenstein, Austria
Arnoldstein, Austria

Baška Grapa (It.: valle del Baccia), Slovenia (v)
Baško sedlo or Rindloch (Ge.: Bačapass, It.: Forcella del Bove or Sella Baccia), Slovenia (p)
Begunje, (Ge.: Vigaun), Slovenia
Belica or Belca, near Dovje, Slovenia
Bistrica (Ge.: Feistritz?), near Črnomelj, Slovenia
Bitnje (Ge.: Wittach), Slovenia
Bled (Ge.: Veldes), Slovenia
Bogatinsko sedlo (Ge.: Bogatin-Sattel, It.: Passo Bogatin), near Ukanc, Slovenia (p)
Bohinj (Ge.: Wochein or Wocheiner-Tal), Slovenia (v)
Bohinjska Bela (Ge.: Wocheiner-Vellach), Slovenia
Bohinjska Bistrica (Ge.: Wocheiner-Feistritz), Slovenia
Bohinjska Češnjica, (Ge.: Kerschdorf), Slovenia
Bohinjsko jezero (Ge.: Wocheinersee), Slovenia
Bohinjsko sedlo (It.: Sella Bochinisa), near Sorica, Slovenia (p)
Bohinjski predor (Ge.: Wocheiner-Tunnel, It.: Galleria di Piedicolle), Slovenia
Brenner (It.: valico del Brennero), between Austria and Italy (p)
Bresoutz, (unidentified locality) between Arnoldstein and Alt-Finkenstein, Austria
Brod (Ge.: Fürten), near Bohinjska Bistrica, Slovenia

Celje (Ge.: Cilli), Slovenia

Cerkno (Ge.: Kirchheim, It.: Circhina), Slovenia

Čez Suho, near Stržišče, Slovenia (p)

Coccau (Ge.: Goggau), Italy

Črnomelj (Ge.: Tschernembl), Slovenia

Davča (Ge.: Dautscha), Slovenia

Dobrava (Ge.: Dobrawa), near Bohinjska Bistrica, Slovenia

Dom Krnica or Koča v Krnici, locality of Krnica near Kranjska Gora, Slovenia (h)

Dom na Komni (Ge.: Komna-Haus), near Ukanc, Slovenia (h)

Dovška Planina, near Dovje, Slovenia

Dovje (Ge.: Langenfeld in Oberkrain), Slovenia

Draschitz, Austria

Dreiländereck (It.: cippo Tre Confini, Sl.: Tromeja), between Austria, Italy, and Slovenia

Erjavčeva koča na Vršiču, near Kranjska Gora, Slovenia (h)

Faak am See, Austria

Feistritz an der Gail, Austria

Feistritzer Alm, near Feistritz an der Gail, Austria

Fiume (Cr.: Rijeka), Croatia

Fürstenfeld, Austria

Fusine in Valromana (Ge.: Weissenfels), Italy

Fužine, Slovenia

Globoko (It.: Passo Globoca), Slovenia (p)

Goritschach, Austria

Goritschacher Alm, near Truppe, Austria

Gorizia (Ge.: Görz), Italy

Gorjuše (Ge.: Goriusch), Slovenia

Gosdorf, Austria

Gozd Martuljek (Ge.: Wald in Oberkrain), Slovenia

Grad Impoljca (Ge.: Schloss Neustein), near Studenec, Slovenia

Grad Krumperk (Ge.: Schloss Kreutberg), Slovenia

Grahovo ob Bači (It.: Gracova Serravalle), Slovenia

Granica, (area of Rovti?) near Bohinjska Bistrica, Slovenia

Greuth, near Faak am See, Austria

Grosuplje (Ge.: Grosslup), Slovenia

Hermagor, Austria
Hohenthurn, Austria
Hotavlje (Ge.: Hotaule), Slovenia

Jesenica (It.: Gesenizza), near Cerkno, Slovenia
Jesenice (Ge.: Assling), Slovenia

Kamnje (Ge.: Steinfeld), Slovenia
Kamnik (Ge.: Stein in Oberkrain), Slovenia
Klagenfurt, Austria
Krnica, near Kranjska Gora, Slovenia (v)
Koča na Gozdu pod Vršičem (Ge.: Waldhaus), near Kranjska Gora, Slovenia (h)
Koča pri Savici, near Ukanc, Slovenia (h)
Koča pri Triglavskih jezerih (Ge.: Triglavseen-Hütte), near Ukanc, Slovenia (h)
Kočevje (Ge.: Gottschee), Slovenia
Komna, near Ukanc, Slovenia
Koprivnik v Bohinju (Ge.: Kopriunik), Slovenia
Kranj (Ge.: Krainburg), Slovenia
Kranjska Gora (Ge.: Kronau), Slovenia
Krško (Ge.: Gurkfeld), Slovenia

Laški Rovt (Ge.: Welschgereuth), Slovenia
Latschach, Austria
Ledenitzen, Austria
Leoben, Austria
Lepence (Ge.: Lepenc), near Bohinjska Bistrica, Slovenia
Lienz, Austria
Ljubljana (Ge.: Laibach, It.: Lubiana), Slovenia
Luknja (Ge.: Luknjapass, It.: Passo del Forame), Slovenia (p)

Mala Pišnica (Ge.: Kleinen Pischentza), near Kranjska Gora, Slovenia (v)
Mallestig, near Finkenstein am Faaker See, Austria
Mallestiger Alm, near Illitsch, Austria
Majdelc (Ge.: Meidlitschbauer?), near Podporezen, Slovenia
Maria Elend, Austria
Maribor (Ge.: Marburg an der Drau), Slovenia
Mencingerjeva Koča (Ge.: Menzingerbauer?), near Ravne v Bohinju, Slovenia (h)
Mihov dom na Vršiču, Kranjska Gora, Slovenia (h)
Miklarji (Ge.: Brunngereuth), near Črnomelj, Slovenia
Mojstrana (Ge.: Meistern), Slovenia

Nemška Loka (Ge.: Detschau), Slovenia

Nemški Rovt (Ge.: Deutschgereuth), Slovenia

Nemški Rut (Ge.: Deutschruth, It.: Rutte di Gracova), Slovenia

Nomenj (Ge.: Neuming), Slovenia

Novaki (It.: Novacchi), near Cerkno, Slovenia

Orožnova koča na planini Za Liscem pod Črno prstjo, near Ravne v Bohinju, Slovenia (h)

Panier (-Alm), near Alt-Finkenstein, Austria

Passo di Colle Pietro or Pachmann, near Petrovo Brdo, Slovenia (p)

Petrovo Brdo (Ge.: Petersberg, It.: Colle Pietro), Slovenia

Planina Bareča dolina, near Laški Rovt, Slovenia

Planina Mežakla (Ge.: Muschakla), near Mojstrana, Slovenia

Planina Strmne (Ge.: Strümpe-Alm?), near Nemški Rovt, Slovenia

Planina Uskovnica, near Srednja vas v Bohinju, Slovenia

Planinski dom Tamar, near Rateče-Planica, Slovenia (h)

Planinsko Društvo Peč 1509, near Rateče-Planica, Slovenia (h)

Plašajtar (Ge.: Plaschaiter), near Podporezen, Slovenia

Podbrdo (It.: Piedicolle), Slovenia

Podhočar (Ge.: Hotsch?), near Podporezen, Slovenia

Podkluže (Ge.: Podkusche), near Mojstrana, Slovenia

Podkoren (Ge.: Wurzen), Slovenia

Podporezen (Ge.: Podporsen), Slovenia

Podrošt (Ge.: Rostberg), Slovenia

Pod Šavnikom, near Bohinjska Bistrica, Slovenia

Pola (Cr.: Pula), Croatia

Poljane (Ge.: Pölan), near Spodnje Gorje, Slovenia

Polje (Ge.: Feld), near Bohinjska Bistrica, Slovenia

Poštarski dom na Vršiču, near Kranjska Gora, Slovenia (h)

Prehod, near Srednja vas v Bohinju, Slovenia

Prelaz Vršič (Ge.: Mojstrovkapass/Werschetzpass, It.: Passo della Moistrocca), Slovenia (p)

Pri Zagi, near Podporezen, Slovenia

Pridou (-Hütte), near Arneutz, Austria (h)

Radovljica (Ge.: Radmannsdorf), Slovenia

Rateče-Planica (Ge.: Ratschach-Matten or Ratschach-Alpen), Slovenia

Ravne v Bohinju (Ge.: Raune), Slovenia

Ravne, near Podrošt, Slovenia

Rečica (Ge.: Retschitz), near Bled, Slovenia

Riegersdorf-Tschau, Austria

Robar, near Podbrdo, Slovenia

Rosenbach, Austria

Rotkar, near Sorica, Slovenia

Rovtar, (Ge.: Rauterbauer?), near Podporezen, Slovenia

Rovti, near Ravne v Bohinju, Slovenia

Savica (Ge.: Savitza or Sawitz), near Bohinjska Bistrica, Slovenia

Schnabl (-Heustadel), near Feistritz an der Gail, Austria

Seltschach, Austria

Senožeta, near Srednja vas v Bohinju, Slovenia

Slap Savica, near Ukanc, Slovenia

Slugov grič or Slugova dolina (It.: Passo di Sluga), near Cerkno, Slovenia (p)

Sorica (Ge.: Zarz), Slovenia

Soriška Planina (It.: Malghe di Sora), Slovenia

Spodnje Gorje (Ge.: Unter-Göriach), near Bled, Slovenia

Srednja vas v Bohinju (Ge.: Mitterdorf in Wochein), Slovenia

Srednji vrh (Ge.: Mitterberg bei Wald), near Gozd Martuljek, Slovenia

Spodnje Danje (Ge.: Unter-Daine), Slovenia

Štadler (Ge.: Stadler), near Sorica, Slovenia

Stara Fužina (Ge.: Althammer), Slovenia

Stara Oselica (Ge.: Altosslitz), Slovenia

Stična (Ge.: Sittich), Slovenia

Stryj, Ucraina

Stržišče (It.: Sant'Osvaldo), near Grahovo ob Bači, Slovenia

Studor v Bohinju (Ge.: Studorf), Slovenia

Sv. Janez (Ge.: St. Johann am Wocheinersee), near Ribčev Laz, Slovenia

Tamar, near Rateče-Planica, Slovenia (v)

Tarvisio (Ge.: Tarvis), Italy

Thörl-Maglern, Austria

Töbring, Austria

Torka, near Podrošt, Slovenia

Tičarjev dom, locality of Trenta near Soča, Slovenia (h)

Trata (Ge.: Tratten), near Gorenja vas, Slovenia

Triglavski dom na Kredarici (Ge.: Kredarica-Hütte), Mount Triglav, Slovenia (h)

Trojar (Ge.: Tojar?), near Podrošt, Slovenia

Ukanc (Ge.: Ukanca or Ukanz), Slovenia

Velika Pišnica (Ge.: Großen Pischentza), near Kranjska Gora, Slovenia (v)

Villach (It.: Villaco), Austria

Vodnikov dom na Velem polju (Ge.: Vodnik-Hütte), Mount Triglav, Slovenia (h)

Vogar (Ge.: Voga-Alpe?), Stara Fužina, Slovenia

Voje, near Stara Fužina, Slovenia

Vrata (Ge.: Vrata-Tal), near Mojstrana, Slovenia (v)

Woroutz, near Unteraichwald, Austria

Wurzenpass (Sl.: Korensko sedlo), between Austria and Slovenia (p)

Zabrdo, near Podrošt, Slovenia

Zali Log (Ge.: Salilog), Slovenia

Zgornje Danje (Ge.: Ober-Daine), Slovenia

Zgornja Radovna (Ge.: Ober-Rothwein), Slovenia

Žiri (Ge.: Sairach), Slovenia

Žlan (Ge.: Schlan), Slovenia

APPENDIX IX
Abbreviations

Abt.	Abteilung
ARAR	Arolsen Archives, Bad Arolsen
ARS	Arhiv Republike Slovenije, Ljubljana
ASU	Archivio di Stato, Udine
ASV	Archivio di Stato, Varese
Ausg.	Ausgabe
BA	Bundesarchiv, Berlin
BA-MA	Bundesarchiv Militärarchiv, Freiburg im Breisgau
BdO	Befehlshaber der Ordnungspolizei
BdS	Befehlshaber der Sicherheitspolizei und des SD
BefSt	Befehlsstelle
BZKom (G)	Bezirkszollkommissar (G) / Bezirkszollkommissariat (G)
BZKom (St)	Bezirkszollkommissar (St) / Bezirkszollkommissariat (St)
Fl.	Folge
FSBB	Führungsstab für Bandenbekämpfung
GASt	Grenzaufsichtsstelle
Gestapo	Geheime Staatspolizei
GÜSt	Grenzübergangsstelle
GZSt	Grenzzollstelle
HZA	Hauptzollamt (G)
HSSPF	Höherer SS- und Polizeiführer
INZ	Inštitut za novejšo zgodovino, Ljubljana
KdS	Kommandeur der Sicherheitspolizei und des SD
KLA	Kärntner Landesarchiv, Klagenfurt
KvK II. Kl. m. Schw.	Kriegsverdienstkreuz II. Klasse mit Schwertern
NARA	National Archives and Records Administration, Washington
OeStA	Österreichisches Staatsarchiv, Vienna
OFPräs	Oberfinanzpräsident / Oberfinanzpräsidium
ÖNB	Österreichischen Nationalbibliothek, Vienna
OZAK	Operationszone Adriatisches Küstenland
Pkt.	Punkt
RSHA	Reichssicherheitshauptamt
SD	Sicherheitsdienst
Sipo	Sicherheitspolizei
St.	Stück
Stp.	Stützpunkt

t.e.	tehnična enota
VGAD	Verstärkter Grenzaufsichtsdienst
ZAL ŠKL	Zgodovinski Arhiv Ljubljana, Škofja Loka
ZASt (G)	Zollaufsichtsstelle (G)
ZASt (St)	Zollaufsichtsstelle (St)
z.b.V.	zur besonderen Verwendung
ZGSch.	Zollgrenzschutz
(Cr.:)	Croatian
(E)	Eisenbahnzollamt
(G)	mit Grenze
(Ge.:)	German
(h)	Alpine hut
(It.:)	Italian
(L)	Landstraßenzollamt / Straßenzollamt
(P)	Abteilung Personal und Verwaltung
(p)	Alpine pass
(Sl.:)	Slovenian
(St)	Steuer
(Z)	Abteilung Zoll

Endnotes

Chapter 1

1. The Reichsfinanzverwaltung was structured on three levels: the *Reichsminister der Finanzen*, the *Oberfinanzpräsident* (midlevel), and the *Vorsteher des Finanzamts / Vorsteher des Hauptzollamts* and their subordinated offices (lower level). The *Reichsminister der Finanzen* was at the same time head of the Reichsfinanzverwaltung and the Reichsfinanzministerium. For an in-depth analysis of the extensive responsibilities and activities of the Reichsfinanzverwaltung, here only briefly mentioned, see BA, R 2, R 110, and R 110 Anh.; Karl Groth, *Der Reichsfinanzverwaltung* (Berlin and Vienna: Industrieverlag Spaeth & Linde, 1942–1944). Specifically on the history and organizational structure of the Zollgrenzschutz-VGAD, see BA, R 2/29795, no heading, *Aufbau der Zollverwaltung*, no date, and R 110/01, unfinished handbook for the Zollgrenzschutz; Walter Eulitz, *Die Geschichte des Zollgrenzdienstes (Der Zollgrenzdienst)* (Bonn, Germany: Wilhelm Stollfuß Verlag, 1968), 102–235.

2. For this reason, from now on, the units of the Zollgrenzschutz-VGAD will be indicated, for simplicity, as Zollgrenzschutz. Also, the term "border guards" will be used to indicate the members of the Zollgrenzschutz-VGAD.

3. The term "mit Grenze," often abbreviated in (G), indicated the Reichsfinanzverwaltung offices located in regions affected by the presence of the Reichsgrenze, which were also in charge of controlling the border. In internal communications, for simplicity, the (G) was usually omitted from the office denominations, with the exception of the cases relating to the BZKom (G) and ZASt (G). The term "Steuer," often abbreviated in (St), indicated the departments specifically responsible for taxes.

4. The isolated areas, rural or Alpine, which extended in between two border crossings within a Grenzabschnitt, were indicated by the colloquial term of "Grüne-Grenze" ("green border"). BA, R 19/464, Der Reichsführer-SS und Chef der Deutschen Polizei im Reichsministerium des Innern, *Polizeigrenze gegenüber dem Protektorat*, 13.08.1941.

5. When the designation "GASt" was used, and when ZASt (G), is not clear. According to some sources, during the war, with border control having become more important than customs-related tasks, the term "ZASt (G)" was abandoned. Nevertheless, as we will see, within the areas subordinated to the territorial jurisdiction of the Hauptzollamt Villach, the designations GASt and ZASt (G) continued to be used at the same time until the end of the war.

6. By 1941, some Zollgrenzschutz members operated in close contact with the Grenzpolizei (border police), a branch of the Geheime Staatspolizei (Gestapo or Stapo; Secret State Police). The Gestapo belonged to the Sicherheitspolizei (Sipo; security police), which, along with the Sicherheitsdienst (SD; intelligence service of the SS), was the backbone of the Reichssicherheitshauptamt (RSHA; national department of security of the Reich). Until the creation of Gruppe IV G in late 1944, matters relating to the Grenzpolizei within the Amt IV (Gegnerforschung und Gegnerbekämpfung) of the RSHA—also known as Geheime Staatspolizeiamt—were mainly dealt by offices IV E 1, IV F 1, IV F 2, and IV A 3 c. The staff of the Grenzpolizei, which was rather limited, principally carried out police activities for the security of the state at the

Reich's principal border crossings and had priority for the "Paßkontrolle" (passports control) over the Zollgrenzschutz, which dealt with this task only in the absence of the Grenzpolizei. The Grenzpolizei was organized into *Grenzpolizeikommissariat* (border police commissariats), which were in turn made up of a network of *Grenzpolizeiposten* (border police posts). The *Grenzpolizeikommissariat* were usually put under control of the IV 3 c office within the Gestapo main centers "mit Grenze" (usually a *Staatspolizeileitstelle* or *Staatspolizeistelle*, but sometimes also a Kommandeur der Sipo/SD). On the collaboration between Zollgrenzschutz and Grenzpolizei, see Walter Eulitz, *Die Geschichte des Zollgrenzdienstes (Der Zollgrenzdienst)* (Bonn, Germany: Wilhelm Stollfuß Verlag, 1968), 105–108 and 235–236; and Thomas Sandkühler, "Von der 'Gegnerabwehr' zum Judenmord: Grenzpolizei und Zollgrenzschutz im NS-Staat," in *"Durchschnittstäter"—Handeln und Motivation*, Beiträge zur Geschichte des Nationalsozialismus 16 (Assoziation Schwarze Risse-Rote Straße, 2000). On the Gestapo and the Grenzpolizei, see also Hans Buchheim, *SS und Polizei im NS-Staat* (Duisdorf, Germany: Studiengesellschaft für Zeitprobleme, 1964); and Supreme Headquarters Allied Expeditionary Forces–Evaluation and Dissemination section, G-2 (Counter Intelligence Subdivision), *The German Police* (London: Supreme Headquarters Allied Expeditionary Forces, 1945), 52, 55, 60–61.

7. Regarding the organizational structure of Gruppe IV G (Dienststelle des Generalgrenzinspekteurs) of the RSHA, information is very scarce. Also referred to as Referat IV G, it was created during the autumn of 1944 and was formed by several main offices; among them, certainly the one of the Inspekteur des Zollgrenzschutzes and at least the ones referred to as IV G 1, 2 and 3, whose responsibilities still remain unknown. As for the *Grenzreferat* departments of the Oberfinanzpräsidium (G), according to the joint order of the *Reichsminister der Finanzen / Reichsführer-SS* dated October 30, 1944, they were supposed to be integrated within the Referat IV G of their local Sipo/SD commanders' offices (Inspekteur or Befehlshaber der Sipo/SD). In regard to most of the *Dienststelle* and the staff of the Zollgrenzschutz, they were apparently subordinated, within the IV G offices of their respective local Gestapo main centers "mit Grenze" (usually a *Staatspolizeileitstelle* or a Kommandeur der Sipo/SD, but in some cases also a Befehlshaber der Sipo/SD), to a department referred to as "Abteilung Zollgrenzschutz" or "Grenzschutz." No detailed information could be found so far regarding the organizational structure of the Grenzpolizei in this context. On these topics, see ARS, SI AS 2175, t.e. 17, Der Generalgrenzinspekteur–IV G 2 a, *Ausbildung von Zollhundführern und Zollhunden*, 30.10.1944; ibid., RSHA–Der Generalgrenzinspekteur–IV G 3, *An alle Staatspolizei(leit)stellen und Kommandeure der Sipo/SD mit Grenze*, 06.01.1945; ibid., BdS Salzburg–Der Grenzreferent, *Meldungen von Angehörigen des Zollgrenzschutzes zur Waffen-SS bzw. zur Wehrmacht*, 19.01.1945; ASV, ZGSch. Italien–BZKom (G) Varese, box 2, folder 15, Der Generalgrenzinspekteur–IV G 2 a 1, *Entschädigung für Futterunkosten während der Aufzucht von Welpen*, 20.11.1944, and Der Generalgrenzinspekteur–IV G 2 a, *Hundezucht*, 27.02.1945; BA, R 110 Anh./6, Der Chef der Sipo/SD-Der Generalgrenzinspekteur-IV G 1 b, *Zollgrenzschutzanordnung Nr. 18*, 07.10.1944 and BdS im Generalgouvernement–Kommandostelle des Zollgrenzschutzes, *Abdruck zur Kenntnis und Beachtung*, 20.11.1944; ibid., R 110 Anh./18, Der Reichsminister der Finanzen/Der Reichsführer-SS, *Richtlinien für die*

Überführung des Zollgrenzschutzes in den Dienstbereich des Reichsführers-SS, 30.10.1944; Central Intelligence Agency, Nazi War Disclosure Act, 2001–2008, Declassified and Released Dispatch nr. EGQW-4804 (Generalmajor der Polizei Otto Somann), 03.03.1953; and NARA, T 175, R 20, frame 2525177, Der Reichsführer-SS, *SS-Befehl*, 31.07.1944 and T 501, R 218, frame 000675-000676, BdS im Generalgouvernement, *Übernahme des Zollgrenzschutzes in die Sicherheitspolizei*, 18.09.1944.

Chapter 2

1. As a consequence of this change, the Karawankengrenze was transformed, for a certain period, in Polizeigrenze, which is a Reich internal border subjected to police control. In 1943, it was generically indicated as "Grenzverlauf zwischen dem Deutschen Reich und dem unter deutscher Zivilverwaltung stehenden Gebiet." ARS, SI AS 1622, t.e. 20, Gendarmeriekreis Radmannsdorf, *Antrag auf Austausch für die Polizeigrenze*, 22.11.1941; BA, R 19/464, Der Reichsführer-SS und Chef der Deutschen Polizei im Reichsministerium des Innern, *Aufhebung der Polizeigrenze gegenhüber Oberkrain*, 27.10.1942; Karte der Alpen- und Donau-Reichsgaue (Reichsgaue Wien, Niederdonau, Oberdonau, Salzburg, Tirol mit Vorlarlberg, Kärnten und Steiermark), Maßstab 1:500000, Hauptvermessungsabteilung XIV Wien, Ausgabe IV. 1943; and Marjan Linasi, Die Kärntner Partisanen (Klagenfurt, Austria: Mohorjeva/Hermagoras, 2010), 19.

2. For military and political reasons, in January 1942 Rösener issued an order by which the civilian transit at the border crossings of the Kreis Radmannsdorf was permitted only through the first-category crossings of Fusine/Rateče and Bohinjska Bistrica (likely to be understood as the Wocheiner-Tunnel or Bohinjski predor, the railway tunnel of Bohinjska Bistrica-Podbrdo, which connected the Kreis Radmannsdorf with the Provincia di Gorizia). In order to cross the border in this sector, along with the passport it was required to show the "Grenzübertrittschein Süd" (pass for the Reich's southern border) or a special permit of the HSSPF im Wehrkreis XVIII. In October 1943, all border crossings with Italy were forbidden to nonmilitary traffic. ARS, SI AS 1605, t.e. 47, Der Gauleiter von Kärnten als Beauftragter des Reichsführer-SS-Reichskommissar für die Festigung deutschen Volkstum Veldes, *Bericht über die Durchführung der Räumung des Grenzstreifens in Oberkrain*, 13.06.1942; Der Beauftragte des Reichskommissars für die Festigung deutschen Volkstums Radmannsdorf, *Räumung des Grenzstreifens*, 05.04.1943; ibid., SI AS 2175, t.e. 17, OFPräs Graz, *An die Herren Vorsteher der Hauptzollämter Krainburg Villach und Cilli*, 13.05.1944; ÖNB, *Alpenländische Rundschau*, Jahrg. 20, Fl. 41, 09.10.1943, p. 5, and *Verordnungs- und Amtsblatt des Chefs der Zivilverwaltung in den besetzten Gebieten Kärntens und Krains*, Ausg. B, Jahrg. 1942, St. 23, 06.11.1942, pp. 192–194; and ZAL-ŠKL, 0268, 79, OK-C-15, HSSPF im Wehrkreis XVIII, *Bekanntmachung–Objava*, 20.01.1942.

3. Concerning the annexation of Gorenjska and the creation of Oberkrain, see Tone Ferenc, *Nacistična raznarodovalna politika v Sloveniji v letih 1941–1945* (Maribor, Slovenia: 1968), 138–151; Tone Ferenc, "Okupacijski sistemi med drugo svetovno vojno 1," in *Historia*, Oddelka za zgodovino Filosofske fakultete Univerze v Ljubljani, Nr. 12 (Ljubljana, Slovenia: 2006), 482–487; and ÖNB, *Verordnungs- und Amtsblatt des Chefs der Zivilverwaltung für die/in den besetzten Gebieten Kärntens und Krains*,

1942–1945. Concerning the OZAK creation, see Stefano Di Giusto, *Operationszone Adriatisches Küstenland* (Udine, Italy: IFSML, 2005), 57–66. About the Italian-Yugoslav border ("Rapallo border"), see ÖNB, Jos. Jul. Schätz, *Zeitschrift des Deutschen und Österreichischen Alpenvereins* (Munich: Verlag F. Bruckmann, 1942), 131–143; Peter Mikša and Matija Zorn, "Rapalska meja: Četrt stoletja obstoja in stoletje dediščine," in *Historia*, Oddelka za zgodovino Filosofske fakultete Univerze v Ljubljani, Nr. 25 (Ljubljana, Slovenia: 2018), 605–641; and Vittorio Adami, *Storia documentata dei Confini del Regno d'Italia* (Rome: Istituto Poligrafico dello Stato, 1931), 136–140.

Chapter 3

1. ARS, SI AS 1622, t.e. 19, Gendarmerie-Hochgebirgsposten Wocheiner-Feistritz, *Kurzmeldung*, 15.11.1944; ibid., SI AS 1931, t.e. 756, Der Kommandant des Schutzgebietes Untersteiermark, *Sonderbefehl über Einrichtung von Schutzgebieten und Sicherungsabschnitten*, 15.02.1945; ibid., t.e. 825, HSSPF im Wehrkreis XVIII-FSBB-Ia, *Befehl zu Befriedung von Oberkrain und Untersteiermark*, 21.12.1943; ibid., t.e. 828, Der Beauftragte des HSSPF im Wehrkreis XVIII für die Bandenbekämpfung in Untersteiermark, *Sonderbefehl über Einrichtung von Schutzgebieten und Sicherungsabschnitten*, 14.09.1944; BA, R 43 II/1348a, Der Reichsminister und Chef der Reichskanzlei, *Zollgrenzschutz in Oberkrain*, 30.01.1942; KLA, AT-KLA 522-8, folder 10, *Tägliche Lageberichte des Kommandeurs der Gendarmerie beim Reichsstatthalter in Kärnten*, 31.08.1944; NARA, T 77 R 748, frame 1981977, HSSPF im Wehrkreis XVIII–FSBB, *Sonderbefehl Nr. 1*, 08.08.1944; Tone Ferenc, "Okupacijski sistemi med drugo svetovno vojno 1," in *Historia*, Oddelka za zgodovino Filosofske fakultete Univerze v Ljubljani, Nr. 12 (Ljubljana, Slovenia: 2006), 463–464 and 469–470; and Josef Rausch, *Der Partisanenkampf in Kärnten im Zweiten Weltkrieg* (Vienna: ÖBV 1994), 5–26.

2. According to the *Amtsblatt der Reichsfinanzverwaltung* (the official gazette of the Reichsfinanzverwaltung), the position of Vorsteher des HZA Villach was occupied, since November 1938, by Zollrat Karl Kaiser, later *Oberzollrat*, and in November 1939, by Regierungsrat Dr. Siegfrid Nestler. According to other sources, in September 1939, Nestler was instead involved with the Zollgrenzschutz in Cracow (Generalgouvernement) and in November 1940 was appointed *Grenzreferent* of the Oberfinanzpräsidium Saarbrücken (Westmark). So, it remains inexplicable how, again according to the *Amtsblatt der Reichsfinanzverwaltung*, Regierungsrat Nestler was apparently still holding the position of Vorsteher des HZA Villach in January 1944.

3. About the organizational structures of the Oberfinanzpräsidium Graz and the HZA Villach, see ARS, SI AS 1931, t.e. 825, HSSPF im Wehrkreis XVIII-FSBB-Ia, *Befehl zu Befriedung von Oberkrain und Untersteiermark*, 21.12.1943; ibid., SI AS 2175, t.e. 15, BdO Alpenland-BefSt Veldes-Ia, *Sonderbefehl Nr. 15* and *20*, respectively dated 20.08 and 02.09.1942; ibid., t.e. 17, BdO Alpenland-BefSt Veldes, *Standortverzeichnis* (HZA Villach in Oberkrain and HZA Krainburg), 07.05.1942; ibid., Der Reichsminister der Finanzen, *Beförderungen von Zollgrenzschutzreservisten*, 28.06.1943; ibid., BdO Alpenland-BefSt Veldes, *Bericht über Grosseinsatz am Sairachberg vom 2. bis 4.8.1943*, 09.08.1943; ibid., 188. Res.Geb.Div. (v. Hösslin), *Abschrift!*, 19.04.1944; ibid., OFPräs

Graz, *An die Herren Vorsteher der Hauptzollämter*, 13.05.1944; BA, R 2/9862, no heading, *Nachweisung 3 über beamteneigene Personenkraftwagen und Krafträder*, no date; ibid., R 2/22649, OFPräs Graz, *Übersicht*, 26.02.1944; ibid., R 2/31962, OFPräs Graz, *Baugelände für das Hauptzollamtgebäude in Villach*, 01.08.1939; ibid., R 2/56246, OFPräs Graz, *Lehrer für das Zollhundewesen*, 06.07.1944; ibid., R 2/116887, *Amtsblatt der Reichsfinanzverwaltung*, Jahrg. 24, 14.02.1942, Nr. 4, p. 38, Jahrg. 24, 30.05.1942, Nr. 19, p. 220, Jahrg. 24, 07.08.1942, Nr. 33, p. 312, Jahrg. 24, 26.09.1942, Nr. 41, p. 373; ibid., R 2/123179, *Amtsblatt der Reichsfinanzverwaltung*, Jahrg. 25, 04.03.1943, Nr. 9, p. 76; ibid., R 2/123180, *Amtsblatt der Reichsfinanzverwaltung*, Jahrg. 26, 31.12.1944, Nr. 2, pp. 12–14, Jahrg. 26, 01.04.1944, Nr. 18, p. 77, Jahrg. 26, 01.06.1944, Nr. 31, p. 133, Jahrg. 26, 15.07.1944, Nr. 36, p. 168; ibid., R 110 Anh./10, correspondence between Zollinspektor Karl Dressendörfer and Finanzpräsident Dr. Walter Eulitz, 28.12.1962; ibid., R 110 Anh./14, correspondence between Oberregierungsrat Robert Spieß and Finanzpräsident Dr. Walter Eulitz, 19.04.1963; ibid., R 110 Anh./17, folder Untersteiermark-Krain; BA-MA, RH 7/1816, Oberkommando des Heeres, *Verleihungsliste für Verleihung des KvK 2. Kl. m. Schw.*, 30.01, 20.04, and 01.09.1942; KLA, AT-KLA 39-C-18.301, 18.394, 18.1072, 18.1081, 18.1144, 18.1147, 18.1164, 18.1221, 18.1262, 18.1298, 18.1301, 18.1302, 18.1319, 18.1328, 18.1330, 18.1346, 18.1362, 18.1454, 18.1488, 18.1508, 18.1532, 18.1575, 18.1583, 18.1587, 18.1595, 18.1645, 18.1670, 18.1689; Goris Archive, VGAD-K Adria-BefSt, *Einsatzbescheinigung*, 06.06.1945 (in copy); ÖNB, *Adressbuch der Stadt Graz 1943/1944*, Jahrg. 66, pp. 53 and 292; ibid., *Alpenländische Rundschau*, Jahrg. 20, Fl. 20, 15.05.1943, p. 5; ibid., *Kärntner Volkszeitung*, Jahrg. 10, Fl. 96, 02.12.1939, p. 9, and Jahrg. 14, Fl. 53, 08.05.1943, p. 4; ibid., *Ostmark-Jahrbuch 1941*, p. 215, and *1942*, p. 228; and Walter Eulitz, *Die Geschichte des Zollgrenzdienstes (Der Zollgrenzdienst)* (Bonn, Germany: Wilhelm Stollfuß Verlag, 1968), 208.

4. Some *Grenzpolizeiposten* also belonged, in various periods, to the organizational structure of the BdS Salzburg within the Kreis Villach and Radmannsdorf. In the Kreis Villach, it has been possible to identify those of Arnoldstein-Bahnhof (with a detachment in Tarvisio, Provincia di Udine) and Thörl-Maglern (at the *Grenzzollstelle* of the border crossing of Coccau/Thörl), both subordinated to the Staatspolizeistelle Klagenfurt through the Grenzpolizeikommissariat Villach. In the Kreis Radmannsdorf, apparently employed at the *Grenzzollstelle*, there were those of the border crossings of Fusine/Rateče (Ratschach-Matten-Zolldienstgebäude) and of the Bohinjski predor tunnel (Wocheiner-Feistritz-Bahnhof); they were both subordinated to the "IV E" office of the KdS Veldes, at least until 1943, through the Grenzpolizeikommissariat Krainburg. According to an unclear source, apparently employed in Bohinjska Bistrica for "customs duty" was also the 3. Zug of the 4. Kompanie/Schutzmannschafts-Bataillon der SD 11, a company formed by Russians and Ukrainians, subordinated to the KdS Veldes and based in Bled. About such posts and units, see ARS, SI AS 1851, t.e. 61, Izdal obveščevalni Oddelek Glavnega Štaba NOV in PO Slovenije, *Podroben opis sovražnih edinic na Teritoriju kontroliranem po NOV in POS*, p. 65; ASU, Corte d'Assise Straordinaria, ED 26, N. del. Reg. Gen. 1/17, Criminal proceedings against Fulgenzio Di Centa, Grenzpolizeiposten Arnoldstein-Aussenstelle Tarvis, *An der Befehlshaber der Sicherheitspolizei und des SD in der Operationszone "Adriatisches*

Küstenland," 10.04.1945; author's archive, *Dienststellenverzeichnis der Sipo/SD-KdS für die besetzten Gebiete Kärtens und Krains in Veldes* and *Staatspolizeistelle Klagenfurt,* 19.04.1943 (in copy); Gariup Archive, HSSPF OZAK-Sicherheitskommandant Kanaltal (Tarvis), *Lagebericht,* 12.10.1944 (in copy); and Supreme Headquarters Allied Expeditionary Forces–Evaluation and Dissemination section, G-2 (Counter Intelligence Subdivision), *The German Police* (London: Supreme Headquarters Allied Expeditionary Forces, 1945), F17–F20. About the organizational structures of the Gestapo and Grenzpolizei in the Oberkrain in general, see ARS, SI AS 1931, t.e. 849, *Obmejna Policija Splošno;* Državni Sekretarijat za unutrašnje poslove FNRJ, *Nemačka Obaveštajna Služba* (Belgrade, Yugoslavia: 1957); and Tone Ferenc, "Okupacijski sistemi med drugo svetovno vojno 1," in *Historia,* Oddelka za zgodovino Filosofske fakultete Univerze v Ljubljani, Nr. 12 (Ljubljana, Slovenia: 2006), 461–473.

5. At least since the second half of November 1944, also entrusted to Hahn was the position of commander of the Sicherungsabschnitt III within the Schutzgebiet Oberkrain; the territorial extension of this security sector is not known with certainty, but it is known that it also had its headquarters in Kranj. The Sicherungsabschnitt III was one of eight security sectors that formed the Schutzgebiet Oberkrain. At least two of such sectors were set up in the Kreis Radmannsdorf: Sicherungsabschnitt VII, which had its headquarters in Bled and roughly corresponded to the district ("okrožje") of Radovljica, and Sicherungsabschnitt VIII, which had its seat in Jesenice and roughly corresponded to the Jesenice district. No detailed data are available for the Sicherungsabschnitt of the Schutzgebiet Kärnten. See ARS, SI AS 1622, t.e. 17, Gendarmeriehauptmannschaft Krainburg, *Sonderbefehl,* 16.01.1945; ibid., t.e. 19, Gendarmerieposten Kronau, *Bandenmeldung Nr. 16,* 19.09.1944, and Gendarmerie-Hochgebirgsposten Wocheiner-Feistritz, *Bandenmeldung Nr. 69/44* and *76/44,* respectively dated 10.11 and 27.11.1944; and INZ, Zapuščina Dr. Tone Ferenc, folder 88, Der Kommandant des Schutzgebietes Oberkrain-Sicherungsabschnitt III, *Allen unterstellten Einheiten,* 22.11.1944.

6. Regarding the changes made during the second half of 1944 to the organizational structures of the Grenzreferat Graz and the HZA Villach, see ARS, AS 1931, t.e. 806, BZKom (G) Wocheiner-Feistritz, *Lagebericht März* 1945, 29.03.1945, and BZKom (G) Wocheiner-Feistritz, *Tätigkeitsbericht,* 06.04.1945; ibid., SI AS 2175, t.e. 17, BdS im Wehrkreis XVIII-Der Grenzreferent, *Einberufung zur Bandenkampfschule des HSSPF,* 07.10.1944; ibid., Vorsteher des HZA Villach, *Abschrift!,* 25.10.1944; ibid., BdS Salzburg–Der Grenzreferent für Steiermark und Untersteiermark, no title, 17.11.1944; ibid., BdS Salzburg–Der Grenzreferent, *Waffenbehandlung,* 18.11.1944; ibid., BZKom (G) Laak-West, *Bandenlage,* 05 and 06.12.1944; Leiter d. BefSt d. ZGSch. Villach, *HZAss Albert Sponfelder,* 13.12.1944; ibid., Wehrersatz-Inspektion Graz, *Nachuntersuchung von Männern des Zollgrenzschutzes und Ordungspolizei,* 14.12.1944; ibid., BZKom (G) Wocheiner-Feistritz, *Freigabe des Zollgrenzschutzreservisten Ruschka Leopold,* 15.12.1944; ibid., Leiter d. BefSt d. ZGSch. Villach, *Abschrift,* 18.12.1944; ibid., Leiter d. BefSt d. ZGSch. Villach, *Freigabe von Zollgrenzschutzangehörigen für den Rüstungsstab Kammler,* 21.12.1944; ibid., BdS Salzburg–Der Grenzreferent, *Abschrift zur Kenntnis und Beachtung,* 22.12.1944; ibid., Leiter d. BefSt d. ZGSch. Villach (Abwicklungsstelle), *Je Abschrift*

Herrn BZKom (G) Thörl-Maglern, Kronau, Wocheiner-Feistritz, 28.12.1944; ibid., OFPräs Graz, *St-Sondermittelungen Z am 12.12.1944*, 15.01.1945; ibid., BdS Salzburg–Der Grezreferent, *Meldungen von Angehörigen des Zollgrenzschutzes zur Waffen-SS bzw. zur Wehrmacht*, 19.01.1945; ibid., BZKom (G) Wocheiner-Feistritz, *Abordnung des HZAss Aichmayer*, 24.01.1945; ibid., KdS Veldes–Abt. ZGSch. Oberkrain in Krainburg, *Abdruck zur Beachtung*, 27.01.1945; ibid., BdS Salzburg– Der Grenzreferent, *Abschrift zu Kenntnis*, 29.01 and 01.02.1945; ibid., KdS Veldes, no title, 02.02.1945; ibid., KdS Veldes-Abt. ZGSch. Oberkrain in Krainburg, *Abdruck zur Kenntnis*, 03 and 09.02.1945; ibid., BdS Salzburg–Der Grenzreferent, *Mangelhafte Ausstattung der 1. Einsatzkompanie Donaueschingen*, 03.02.1945; ibid., BZKom (G) Wocheiner-Feistritz, *Wachhunde*, 07.02.1945; ibid., KdS Veldes– Abt. ZGSch. Oberkrain in Krainburg, *Abschrift zur Kenntnisnahme*, 14.02.1945; ibid., BdS Salzburg–Untersuchnungsführer, *Unerlaubte Entfernung*, 17.02.1945; ibid., KdS Veldes–Abt. ZGSch. Oberkrain in Krainburg, *Abgabe von Waffen und Munition*, 26.02.1945; ibid., KdS Veldes–Abt. ZGSch. Oberkrain in Krainburg, *Pfluger*, 26.02.1945; ibid., KdS Veldes–Abt. ZGSch. Oberkrain in Krainburg, *An ZS Georg Stelzer GASt Petersberg*, 05.03.1945; ibid., KdS Veldes–Abt. ZGSch. Oberkrain in Krainburg, *Unterkünfte des Zollgrenzschutzes*, 05.03.1945; ibid., KdS Veldes–Abt. ZGSch. Oberkrain in Krainburg, no title, 06.03.1945; ibid., BZKom (G) Wocheiner-Feistritz, *An HZAss Schneider-Goritschnig*, 12.03.1945; ibid., BZKom (G) Enderlein, "*Niederschrift*" in KdS Veldes–Abt. ZGSch. Oberkrain in Krainburg, *Abschrift zur Kenntnis*, 13.03.1945; ibid., BZKom (G) Wocheiner-Feistritz, *Verleihung des KvK 2. Kl. m. Schw. an Angehörige des Zollgrenzschutzes*, 15.03.1945; ibid., KdS Veldes–Abt. ZGSch. Oberkrain in Krainburg, *Verhalten auf Streifen und Postierungen*, 18.03.1945; ibid., BZKom (G) Wocheiner-Feistritz, *Verwundetenabzeichen*, 20.03.1945; ibid., BZKom (G) Wocheiner-Feistritz, *Anton Valentinisch*, 24.03.1945; ibid., KdS Veldes–Abt. ZGSch. Oberkrain in Krainburg, *Verleihung von KvK 2. Kl. m. Schw.*, 28.03.1945; ibid., SS-u. Polizeigericht XVIII– Zweigstelle Salzburg, *Anklageverfügung und Haftbefehl!*, 31.03.1945; BA, R 2/9862, no heading, *Nachweisung 3 über beamteneigene Personenkraftwagen und Krafträder*, no date; ibid., R 110 Anh./10 and /14, correspondence between Oberregierungsrat Robert Spieß and Finanzpräsident Dr. Walter Eulitz, 19.04.1963; ibid., R 110 Anh./17, folder Untersteiermark-Krain; KLA, AT-KLA 39-C-18.1072, 18.1091 and 18.1301; and OeStA, AdR MilEv ZGS, personal files of Oswald Dellai, Oskar Gaeble, Heinrich Kiefer and Adolf Preiss.

7. ARS, SI AS 2175, t.e. 17, BdO Alpenland-BefSt Veldes, *Standortverzeichnis* (HZA Villach in Oberkrain and HZA Krainburg); and Jože Dežman, *Gorenjski partizan- Gorenjski odred 1942–1944* (Kranj, Slovenia: 1992), 264–265 (organization chart).

8. ARS, SI AS 1851, t.e. 73 (partisan intelligence), *Uradi in postojanke glavnega ca- rinskega urada Hauptzollamt v Kranju/Beljaku*, 1944; ibid., SI AS 2175, t.e. 17, BdO Alpenland–BefSt Veldes, *Standortverzeichnis* (HZA Villach in Oberkrain and HZA Krainburg), 07.05.1942; and ibid., BdO Alpenland, *Ausstattung der Dienststellen des Zollgrenzschutzes mit Leuchtbombenmörser*, 28.06.1943. A list of the BZKom subordinated only to the HZA Villach is also in BA, R 2/25247, OFPräs Graz, *Postanschriften*, 07.04.1944.

9. Since a more widespread use of the designation GASt, in the area under discussion, has been detected compared to that of ZASt (G), the former will be used, for simplicity, to describe the organizational structure of the various BZKom (G) mentioned in the text. In any event, in all cases when the use of the ZASt (G) designation has been found, this will be reported in the in-depth analysis dedicated to a specific BZKom (G).

10. On the organizational structure of the BZKom (G) Arnoldstein, see ARS, SI AS 2175, t.e. 17, BdO Alpenland-BefSt Veldes, *Standortverzeichnis* (HZA Villach in Oberkrain and HZA Krainburg), 07.05.1942; ibid., Vorsteher des HZA Villach, *Herrn BZKom (G) Arnoldstein, Kronau, Wocheiner-Feistritz*, 23.08.1943; BA, R2/28131, *Dienst- und Wohngebäude des Bezirkszollkommissariats Arnoldstein*; ibid., R 2/104789, Reichsfinanzministerium, *Personal-Akten Zollinspektor Karl Müller*; ibid., R 601/2462, Präsidialkanzlei, *Vorschlagsliste für die Verleihung des Zollgrenzschutz-Ehrenzeichens Nr. 4/40, 220/42, 12/43, 20/43*, and *42/43*, respectively dated 19.01.1940, 20.11.1942, and 20.01, 10.02, and 10.03.1943; BA-MA, RH 7/1816, Oberkommando des Heeres, *Verleihungsliste für Verleihung des KvK 2. Kl. m. Schw.*, 30.01, 20.04, and 01.09.1942 and 30.01 and 01.09.1943; KLA, AT-KLA 39-C-18.301, 18.1081, 18.1112, 18.1144, 18.1161, 18.1164, 18.1188, 18.1221, 18.1244, 18.1266, 18.1301, 18.1305, 18.1319, 18.1334, 18.1346, 18.1388, 18.1390, 18.1449, 18.1452, 18.1454, 18.1498, 18.1505, 18.1538, 18.1540, 18.1571, 18.1580, 18.1595, 18.1607, 18.1623, 18.1642, 18.1689, 18.1728, 18.1729; OeStA, AdR MilEv ZGS, personal file of Michael Aigner; and ÖNB, *Adressbuch der Stadt Graz 1943/44*, Jahrg. 66, p. 53.

11. On the organizational structure of the BZKom (G) St. Jakob im Rosental, see BA, R 601/2462, Präsidialkanzlei, *Vorschlagsliste für die Verleihung des Zollgrenzschutz-Ehrenzeichens Nr. 20/43* and *42/43*, respectively dated 10.02 and 10.03.1943; and KLA, AT-KLA 39-C-18.1147, 18.1253, 18.1266, 18.1340, 18.1520, 18.1582, 18.1646.

12. On the organizational structure of the BZKom (G) Obergöriach/Veldes, see ARS, SI AS 1622/II, t.e. 34, Der Kommandeur der Gendarmerie Südkärnten, *Nachrichten über Vorkommnisse in Südkärnten*, 07.01.1942; ibid., SI AS 2175, t.e. 15, BdO Alpenland–BefSt Veldes-Ic, *Informationsdienst Nr. 31* and *42*, respectively dated 02.07 and 04.08.1943; ibid., SI AS 2175, t.e. 17, BdO Alpenland–BefSt Veldes, *Standortverzeichnis* (HZA Villach in Oberkrain and HZA Krainburg), 07.05.1942; ibid., Vorsteher des HZA Villach, *Herrn BZKom (G) Arnoldstein, Kronau, Wocheiner-Feistritz*, 23.08.1943; BA, R 601/2462, Präsidialkanzlei, *Vorschlagsliste für die Verleihung des Zollgrenzschutz-Ehrenzeichens Nr. 12/43, 20/43*, and *42/43*, respectively dated 20.01, 10.02, and 10.03.1943; BA-MA, RH 7/1816, Oberkommando des Heeres, *Verleihungsliste für Verleihung des KvK 2. Kl. m. Schw.*, dated 30.01, 20.04, and 01.09.1942 and 30.01.1943; KLA, AT-KLA 39-C-18.394, 18.1110, 18.1138, 18.1144, 18.1147, 18.1162, 18.1164, 18.1188, 18.1253, 18.1266, 18.1288, 18.1305, 18.1334, 18.1340, 18.1390, 18.1449, 18.1481, 18.1451, 18.1454, 18.1488, 18.1520, 18.1538, 18.1571, 18.1575, 18.1580, 18.1582, 18.1587, 18.1607, 18.1629, 18.1646, 18.1693; ibid., AT-KLA 128-F-H 61, *An "Grünen Grenzen"—Denkwürdigkeiten aus der Dienstzeit im Zollgrenzschutz von Karl Pfister*; ÖNB, *Allgemeine Schutzhütten-Zeitung*, Jahrg. 14, Fl. 9/10, 09./10.1942, p. 12; and Jos. Jul. Schätz, *Zeitschrift des Deutschen und Österreichischen Alpenvereins* (Munich: Verlag F. Bruckmann, 1942), 136 and 140–141.

13. On the organizational structure of the BZKom (G) Kronau, see ARS, SI AS 1622, t.e. 19, Gendarmerieposten Lengenfeld, *Lagebericht von 13. Juli 1943*, 10.07.1943, Gendarmerieposten Kronau, *Bandenmeldung Nr. 25/44*, 25.10.1944, and Gendarmerie-Hochgebirgsposten Legenfeld, *Bandenmeldung Nr. 92/44*, 19.12.1944; ibid., t.e. 24, Gendarmerieposten Legenfeld, *Verzeichnis*, 07.02.1944, and Gendarmerieposten Kronau, *Verzeichnis*, 08.02.1944; ibid., SI AS 1851, t.e. 73 (partisan intelligence), *Uradi in postojanke glavnega carinskega urada Hauptzollamt v Kranju/Beljaku*, 1944; ibid., SI AS 2173, t.e. 48, Gendarmerieposten Kronau, *Fahndung "Alpha"* and *Fahndung "Beta,"* 22.09.1943; ibid., SI AS 2175, t.e. 17, Vorsteher des HZA Villach, *Herrn BZKom (G) Arnoldstein, Kronau, Wocheiner-Feistritz*, 23.08.1943; Vorsteher des HZA Villach, *Abschrift!*, 04.10.1944; ibid., Vorsteher des HZA Villach, *Ausbildungs von Zollhundeführern und Zollhunden in Monat Jänner 1944* (but probably 1945), 21.12.1944; ibid., BdS Salzburg–Der Grenzreferent, *Abschrift zur Kenntnis und Beachtung*, 22.12.1944; ibid., Leiter d. BefSt d. ZGSch. Villach (Abwicklungsstelle), *Je Abschrift Herrn BZKomG Thörl-Maglern, Kronau, Wocheiner-Feistritz*, 28.12.1944; ibid., BZKom (G) Wocheiner-Feistritz, *Personalzugang*, 27.01.1945; ibid., KdS Veldes-Abt. ZGSch. Oberkrain in Krainburg, *Abgabe von Waffen und Munition*, 26.02.1945; ibid., Abt. ZGSch. Oberkrain in Krainburg, no title, 06.03.1945; ibid., BZKom (G) Wocheiner-Feistritz, *An HZAss Schneider-Goritschnig*, 12.03.1945; ibid. BZKom (G) Enderlein, *"Niederschrift"* in KdS Veldes-Abt. ZGSch. Oberkrain in Krainburg, *Abschrift zur Kenntnis*, 13.03.1945; ibid., KdS Veldes-Abt. ZGSch. Oberkrain in Krainburg, *Verleihung von KvK II. Kl. m. Schw.*, 28.03.1945; BA, R 2/9862, no heading, *Nachweisung 3 über beamteneigene Personenkraftwagen und Krafträder*, no date; ibid., R 601/2462, Präsidialkanzlei, *Vorschlagsliste Nr. 20/43 für die Verleihung des Zollgrenzschutz-Ehrenzeichens*, 10.02.1943; BA-MA, RH 7/1816, Oberkommando des Heeres, *Verleihungsliste für Verleihung des KvK 2. Kl. m. Schw.*, 30.01.1943; Jože Dežman, *Gorenjski partizan-Gorenjski odred 1942–1944* (Kranj, Slovenia: 1992), 136–137 (map) and 264–265 (organization chart); KLA, AT-KLA 39-C-18.1065, 18.1072, 18.1091, 18.1112, 18.1138, 18.1161, 18.1188, 18.1221, 18.1244, 18.1253, 18.1288, 18.1301, 18.1305, 18.1330, 18.1334, 18.1337, 18.1452, 18.1454, 18.1541, 18.1570, 18.1582, 18.1583, 18.1593, 18.1597, 18.1625, 18.1632, 18.1642, 18.1646, 18.1660, 18.1699; 18.1723; ibid., AT-KLA 128-F-H 61, *An "Grünen Grenzen"—Denkwürdigkeiten aus der Dienstzeit im Zollgrenzschutz von Karl Pfister*; Mile Pavlin, *Jeseniško Bohinjski Odred* (Ljubljana, Slovenia: Knjižnica NOV in POJ, 1970), 92n1; and ÖNB, *Innsbrucker Nachrichten*, Jahrg. 89, Nr. 62, 14.03.1942, p. 9.

14. On the organizational structure of the BZKom (G) Wocheiner-Feistritz, see ARS, SI AS 1067/III, t.e. 3, *Mrliška knjiga Bohinjska Bistrica* and *Srednja vas v Bohinju*; ibid., SI AS 1622, t.e. 17, Gendarmeriehauptmannschaft Krainburg, *Betrifft: Haus des SS-Gruf. Berger in der Wochein*, 18.06.1943; ibid., t.e. 19, Gendarmerie-Hochgebirgsposten Wocheiner-Feistritz, *Bandenmeldung Nr. 86/44*, 25.12.1944; ibid., t.e. 24, Gendarmerie-Hochgebirgsposten Wocheiner-Feistritz, *Wehrmachts- und Zolldienststellen: Meldung über Bestand und Veränderung*, 09.02.1944; ibid., SI AS 1851, t.e. 73 (partisan intelligence), *Uradi in postojanke glavnega carinskega urada Hauptzollamt v Kranju/Beljaku*, 1944; ibid., SI AS 1931, t.e. 806, BZKom (G) Wocheiner-Feistritz, *Lagebericht März 1945*, 29.03.1945, and *Lagebericht April 1945*, 30.04.1945; ibid., BZKom (G) Wocheiner-Feistritz, *Bandenbewegungen seit dem Pol.Einsatz (20.3.45) im Raume*

Petersberg-Zarz-Kirchheim, 04.04.1945; ibid. BZKom (G) Wocheiner-Feistritz, *Tätigkeitsbericht*, 06 and 13.04.1945; ibid., SI AS 2173, t.e. 38, Gendarmeriekreis Krainburg, *An alle Gendarmeriedienststellen im Kreise*, 25.05.1943; ibid., SI AS 2175, t.e. 15, BdO Alpenland–BefSt Veldes, *Lage*, 15.03.1943, and BdO Alpenland–BefSt Veldes-Ic, *Informationsdienst Nr. 15, 20, 28*, and *47*, respectively dated 15.05, 30.05, 23.06, and 19.08.1943; ibid., t.e. 16, BdO Alpenland–BefSt Veldes-Ic, *Lage am 30. Oktober 1942*, 30.10.1942; ibid., t.e. 17, BdO Alpenland–BefSt Veldes, *Standortverzeichnis* (HZA Villach in Oberkrain and HZA Krainburg), 07.05.1942; ibid., BdO Alpenland, *Ausstattung der Dienststellen des Zollgrenzschutzes mit Leuchtbombenmörser*, 28.06.1943; ibid., BZKom (G) Wocheiner-Feistritz, *Abdruck verteilt*, 25.08.1943; ibid., GASt Zarz, *Zurückhaltung der Lebensmittelkarten wegen Bandengefahr*, 08.12.1943; ibid., Vorsteher des HZA Villach, *Abschrift Herrn BZKom.G Wocheiner-Feistritz*, 12.10.1944; ibid., BZKom (G) Wocheiner-Feinstritz, *Funkgeräte*, 18.10.1944; ibid., BZKom (G) Wocheiner-Feistritz, *Verleihung des KvK 2. Kl. mit Schw. an Angehörige des Zollgrenzschutzes*, 08.12.1944; ibid., BZKom (G), *Vorschlagsliste für die Verleihung des KvK II. Kl. m. Schw.*, 08.12.1944; ibid., Leiter d. BefSt d. ZGSch. Villach, *HZAss Albert Sponfelder*, 13.12.1944; ibid., BZKom (G) Wocheiner-Feistritz, *Freigabe des Zollgrenzschutzreservisten Ruschka Leopold*, 15.12.1944; ibid., Leiter d. BefSt d. ZGSch. Villach, *Anerkennung*, 18.12.1944 (two different documents); ibid., Vorsteher des HZA Villach, *Ausbildung von Zollhundeführern und Zollhunden in Monat Jänner 1944* (but probably 1945), 21.12.1944; ibid., Leiter d. BefSt d. ZGSch. Villach, *Freigabe von Zollgrenzschutzangehörigen für den Rüstungsstab Kammler*, 21.12.1944; ibid., Rudolf Schaffer-Zollinspektor–BZKom (G) Wocheiner-Feistritz, *Verleihungsbestimmungen für das Bandenkampfabzeichen*, 23.01.1945; ibid., BZKom (G) Wocheiner-Feistritz, *Abordnung des HZAss Aichmayer*, 24.01.1945; ibid., BZKom (G) Wocheiner-Feistritz, *Abordnung eines Schuhmachers*, 26.01.1945; ibid., BZKom (G) Wocheiner-Feistritz, *Personalzugang*, 27.01.1945; ibid., BZKom (G) Wocheiner-Feistritz, *Nachtdienstzulagen für Einsatzbesoldungsempfänger*, 05.02.1945; ibid., BZKom (G) Wocheiner-Feistritz, *Wachhunde*, 07.02.1945; ibid., GASt Wocheiner-Feistritz-West, *Meldung*, 13.02.1945; ibid. BZKom (G) Wocheiner-Feistritz, *Vorschlagsliste zur Beförderung von ZGSch Reservisten zu Hilfszollassistenten*, 14.02.1945; ibid., BZKom (G) Wocheiner-Feistritz, *Veränderungsanzeige; Zugänge*, 25.02.1945; ibid., KdS Veldes–Abt. ZGSch. Oberkrain in Krainburg, *Pfluger*, 26.02.1945; ibid., KdS Veldes–Abt. ZGSch. Oberkrain in Krainburg, *An ZS Georg Stelzer GASt Petersberg*, 05.03.1945; ibid., BZKom (G) Wocheiner-Feistritz, *An HZAss Schneider-Goritschnig*, 12.03.1945; ibid., BZKom (G) Enderlein, *"Niederschrift"* in KdS Veldes–Abt. ZGSch. Oberkrain in Krainburg, *Abschrift zur Kenntnis*, 13.03.1945; ibid., GASt Zarz, *Vorschläge zur Verleihung des KvK 2. Kl. m. Schw.*, 13.03.1945; ibid., GASt Petersberg, *Vorschläge zur Verleihung des KvK II. Kl. m. Schw.*, 14.03.1945; ibid., GASt Wocheiner-Feistritz-West, *Vorschläge für die Verleihung des KvK II. Kl m. Schw.*, 14.03.1945; ibid., BZKom (G) Wocheiner-Feistritz, *Verleihung des KvK 2. Kl. m. Schw. an Angehörige des Zollgrenzschutzes*, 15.03.1945; ibid., BZKom (G) Wocheiner-Feistritz, *Vorschlagsliste für die Verleihung des KvK. II. Kl. m. Schw.*, 15.03.1945; ibid., GASt Wocheiner-Feistritz, *Vorschläge von Anträgen zur Verleihung des KvK II. Kl m. Schw.*, 15.03.1945; ibid., BZKom (G) Wocheiner-Feistritz, *Lebensmittelzulage für Nachtarbeiter*, 21.03.1945; ibid., BZKom (G) Wocheiner-Feistritz, *Veränderungsanzeige in der Personalbesetzung*,

23 and 24.03.1945; ibid., BZKom (G) Wocheiner-Feistritz, *Anton Valentinisch*, 24.03.1945; ibid., BZKom (G) Wocheiner-Feistritz, *Abschrift an alle GASten*, 25.03.1945; ibid., KdS Veldes–Abt. ZGSch. Oberkrain in Krainburg, *Verleihung von KvK II. Kl. m. Schw.*, 28.03.1945; ibid., BZKom (G) Wocheiner-Feistritz, *Unterkünfte des Zollgrenzschutzes*, 29.03.1945; ibid., KdS Veldes–Abt. ZGSch. Oberkrain in Krainburg, *Bartheloff*, 31.03.1945; ibid., SS-u. Polizeigericht XVIII–Zweigstelle Salzburg, *Anklageverfügung und Haftbefehl!*, 31.03.1945; ibid., *Stammbuch Nikolaus Blank*; ibid., t.e. 50, Gendarmerie-Hochgebirgsposten Wocheiner-Feistritz, *An die Gestapo-Stapostelle in Bremen*, 24.06.1944; ibid., AS II, Akcesija št. 301, *Nemško vojaško pokopališče Kranj* (Erich Schomaker); BA, R2/9709, OFPräs Graz, *Tempo-Geländekraftwagen*, 16.07.1942 and no heading, *Nachweisung 2 über reichseigene Personenkraftwagen u. reichseigene Krafträder*, no date; ibid., R 2/123179, *Amtsblatt der Reichsfinanzverwaltung*, Jahrg. 25, 04.03.1943, nr. 9, p. 70; BA-MA, RH 7/1816, Oberkommando des Heeres, *Verleihungsliste für Verleihung des KvK 2. Kl. m. Schw.*, 30.01 and 01.09.1943; Deutsches Rotes Kreuz–Suchdienst München, *Vermißtenbildliste* (Munich: 1957), 252; Jože Dežman, *Gorenjski partizan—Gorenjski odred 1942–1944* (Kranj, Slovenia: 1992), 83, 112, 136–137 (map), and 264–265 (organization chart); Mile Pavlin, *Jeseniško Bohinjski Odred* (Ljubljana, Slovenia: Knjižnica NOV in POJ, Partizanska knjiga, 1970), 120 and 126; KLA, AT-KLA 39-C-18.301, 18.394, 18.1110, 18.1112, 18.1138, 18.1147, 18.1161, 18.1162, 18.1164, 18.1188, 18.1200, 18.1218, 18.1221, 18.1288, 18.1298, 18.1302, 18.1305, 18.1319, 18.1328, 18.1334, 18.1340, 18.1341, 18.1393, 18.1431, 18.1451, 18.1488, 18.1505, 18.1514, 18.1520, 18.1527, 18.1529, 18.1532, 18.1541, 18.1562, 18.1563, 18.1574, 18.1576, 18.1583, 18.1593, 18.1597, 18.1629, 18.1642, 18.1646, 18.1670, 18.1689, 18.1704, 18.1732, 18.1743, 18.1747; NARA, RG 498, box 108, interrogation report SO5/USDIC/DC3 (Anton Eder), 11.12.1945; OeStA, AdR MilEv ZGS, personal files of Wilhelm Dannehl, Alois Gaugl, Peter Gössler, Otto Schäfer, Alfred Tannert, Thomas Tscheinig, and Michael Zechner; ÖNB, *Alpenländische Rundschau*, Jahrg. 18, Fl. 38, 20.09.1941, p. 6; and Stanko Petelin, *Gradnikova Brigada* (Ljubljana, Slovenia: Založba borec in revija Naša obramba, 1983), 376.

15. On the organizational structure of the BZKom (G) Thörl-Maglern, see ARS, SI AS 2175, t.e. 17, Vorsteher des HZA Villach, *Abschrift!*, 04.10.1944; ibid., Vorsteher des HZA Villach, *Ausbildungs von Zollhundeführern und Zollhunden in Monat Jänner 1944* (but probably 1945), 21.12.1944; ibid., Leiter d. BefSt d. ZGSch. Villach (Abwicklungsstelle), *Je Abschrift Herrn BZKomG Thörl-Maglern, Kronau, Wocheiner-Feistritz*, 28.12.1944; ibid., BZKom (G) Wocheiner-Feistritz, *Abordnung des HZAss Aichmayer*, 24.01.1945; ibid., BZKom (G) Wocheiner-Feistritz, *Waffen und Geräte aus Mallestig*, 24.01.1945; ibid., BZKom (G) Wocheiner-Feistritz, *ZS. Oberhaus Karl*, 26.01.1945; ibid., BZKom (G) Wocheiner-Feistritz, *Pers. Zugang.*, 30.01.1945; ibid., BZKom (G) Wocheiner-Feistritz, *Lebensmittelzulage für Nachtarbeiter*, 21.03.1945; BA, R 2/9862, no heading, *Nachweisung 3 über beamteneigene Personenkraftwagen und Krafträder*, no date; KLA, AT-KLA 39-C-18.389, 18.1251, 18.1072, 18.1091, 18.1244, 18.1288, 18.1302, 18.1305, 18.1330, 18.1334, 18.1337, 18.1405, 18.1570, 18.1593, 18.1597, 18.1632, 18.1660, 18.1699, 18.1723, 18.1728; ibid., AT-KLA 522-8, folder 10, *Tägliche Lageberichte des KdG beim Reichsstatthalter in Kärnten*, 30.11.1944; and OeStA, AdR MilEv ZGS, personal file of Heinrich Kiefer.

16. On the organizational structure of the BZKom (St) Villach, see BA, R 2/25247, OFPräs Graz, *Postanschriften*, 07.04.1944; ibid., R 2/31962, Vorsteher des HZA Villach, *Stellen- und Raumbedarfsplan für die künftige Unterbringung des Hauptzollamtes und des BZKom Villach*, 24.10.1939; and ÖNB, *Kärntner Volkszeitung*, Jahrg. 10, Fl. 96, 02.12.1939, p. 9.

17. On the *Zollamt* subordinated to the HZA Villach, see ARS, SI AS 1622, t.e. 24, Gendarmerieposten Kronau, *Verzeichnis*, 08.02.1944, and Gendarmerieposten Assling, *Verzeichnis*, 08.02.1944; ibid., SI AS 2173, t.e. 48, Gendarmerieposten Kronau, *Fahndung "Beta,"* 22.09.1943; BA, R 2/104789, Reichsfinanzministerium, *Personal-Akten Zollinspektor Karl Müller*; ibid., R 2/116887, *Amtsblatt der Reichsfinanzverwaltung*, Jahrg. 24, 26.09.1942, Nr. 41, p. 373; ibid., R 601/2433, Präsidialkanzlei, *Vorschlagsliste Nr. 220/42 für die Verleihung des Zollgrenzschutz-Ehrenzeichens*, 20.11.1942; KLA, AT-KLA 39-C-18.1574, 18.1346, 18.1689; ÖNB, *Kärntner Volkszeitung*, Jahrg. 11, Fl. 32, 20.04.1940, p. 8; ibid., *Salzburger Volksblatt*, Jahrg. 69, Fl. 14, 18.01.1939, p. 7; and ibid., *Verordnungs- und Amtsblatt des Chefs der Zivilverwaltung in den besetzten Gebieten Kärntens und Krains*, Jahrg. 1943, St. 8, 29.07.1943, p. 51.

18. On these outposts, see KLA, AT-KLA 128-F-H 61, *An "Grünen Grenzen"—Denkwürdigkeiten aus der Dienstzeit im Zollgrenzschutz von Karl Pfister*; and OeStA, AdR MilEv ZGS, personal file of Thomas Tscheinig.

19. On the Jagdkommando des Zollgrenzschutzes of the Hauptzollamt Villach, see ARS, SI AS 1622, t.e. 19, Gendarmerieposten Lengenfeld, *Lagebericht von 13. Juli 1943*, 10.07.1943, BdO Alpenland–BefSt Veldes-Ia, *Einsatzbefehl Nr. 156*, 15.09.1943, and Gendarmeriekreis Radmannsdorf, *An den BdO Alpenland–BefSt in Veldes*, 16.09.1943; ibid., t.e. 24, Gendarmerieposten Legenfeld, *Verzeichnis*, 07.02.1944; BA, R2/9703, OFPräs Graz, *Dienstkraftwagen*, 06.06.1944; BA-MA, RH 7/1816, Oberkommando des Heeres, *Verleihungsliste für Verleihung des KvK 2. Kl. m. Schw.*, 30.01.1943, and Heerespersonalamt, *Verleihungsliste für Verleihung des KvK 1. Kl. m. Schw.*, 11.09.1944; KLA, AT-KLA 39-C-18.394, 18.1110, 18.1138, 18.1188, 18.1253, 18.1340, 18.1390, 18.1451, 18.1538, 18.1571; ibid., AT-KLA 522-8, folder 10, *Tägliche Lageberichte des Kommandeurs der Gendarmerie beim Reichsstatthalter in Kärnten*, 30.11.1944; and OeStA, AdR MilEv ZGS, personal files of Alois Gaugl and Peter Gössler.

20. On the Ausbildungslager and the Ausweichlager des Zollgrenzschutzes, see ARS, SI 1622, t.e. 17, Gendarmeriehauptmannschaft Krainburg in Veldes, *Auszug aus der Zeitfolge für den Besuch des Herrn Reichsminister der Finanzen, Graf Schwerin von Krosigk, in Oberkrain am 8. und 9. Mai 1943*, 04.05.1943; ibid., SI AS 2175, t.e. 17, Vorsteher des HZA Villach, *Abschrift!*, 04.10.1944; ibid., BdS Salzburg–Der Grenzreferent, *Waffenbehandlung*, 18.11.1944; ibid., BZKom (G) Wocheiner-Feistritz, *Waffen und Geräte aus Mallestig*, 24.01.1945; ibid., BZKom (G) Wocheiner-Feistritz, *Pers. Zugang.*, 30.01.1945; ibid., KdS Veldes–Abt. ZGSch. Oberkrain in Krainburg, no title, 02.02.1945; ibid., GASt Wocheiner-Feistritz-West, *Meldung*, 13.02.1945; ibid., BZKom (G) Wocheiner-Feistritz, *Mangelhafte Ausstattung der Eins.Kp.*, 14.02.1945; ibid., KdS Veldes–Abt. ZGSch. Oberkrain in Krainburg, no title, 06.03.1945; ibid., BZKom (G) Wocheiner-Feistritz, *An HZAss Schneider-Goritschnig*, 12.03.1945; ibid., BZKom (G) Wocheiner-Feistritz, *Lebensmittelzulage für Nachtarbeiter*, 21.03.1945; ibid., SS-u. Polizeigericht XVIII–Zweigstelle Salzburg,

Anklageverfügung und Haftbefehl!, 31.03.1945; BA, R2/22649, OFPräs Graz, *Übersicht*, 26.02.1944; KLA, AT-KLA 39-C-18.1081, 18.1144, 18.1147, 18.1162, 18.1188, 18.1251, 18.1262, 18.1266, 18.1288, 18.1302, 18.1337, 18.1341, 18.1390, 18.1431, 18.1451, 18.1454, 18.1538, 18.1562, 18.1570, 18.1642, 18.1660, 18.1693; and ÖNB, *Kärntner Volkszeitung*, Jahrg. 4, Fl. 54, 10.05.1944, p. 3.

Chapter 4

1. On the training and specialization courses, see ARS, SI AS 1931, t.e. 806, BZKom (G) Wocheiner-Feistritz, *Lagebericht März 1945*, 29.03.1945, and *Lagebericht April 1945*, 30.04.1945; ibid., SI AS 2175, t.e. 17, BdS im Wehrkreis XVIII–Der Grenzreferent, *Einberufung zur Bandenkampfschule des HSSPF*, 07.10.1944; ibid., Vorsteher des HZA Villach, *Abschrift!*, 25.10.1944; ibid., BZKom (G) (Wocheiner-Feistritz), *Vorschlagsliste für die Verleihung des KvK II. Kl. m. Schw.*, 08.12.1944; ibid., BZKom (G) Wocheiner-Feistritz, *Dienstantrittsmeldung*, 02.02.1945; ibid., SS-Ausbildungsabteilung Konitz, *Sonderausweis*, 18.02.1945; ibid., KdS Veldes–Abt. ZGSch. Oberkrain in Krainburg, *Ausbildungslehrgänge*, 23.02.1945; ibid., BZKom (G) Wocheiner-Feistritz, *Veränderungsanzeige; Zugänge*, 25.02.1945; ibid., SS-Stubaf. u. Major der Schupo Pretzell, *Teilnahme-Bescheinigung*, 28.02.1945; ibid., BZKom (G) Wocheiner-Feistritz, *Ausbildungslehrgänge*, 01.03.1945; ibid., KdS Veldes–Abt. ZGSch. Oberkrain in Krainburg, *An ZS Georg Stelzer GASt Petersberg*, 05.03.1945; ibid., BZKom (G) Wocheiner-Feistritz, *Veränderungsanzeige: Abstellung zu Lehrgängen*, 07.03.1945; ibid., KdS Veldes–Abt. ZGSch. Oberkrain in Krainburg, *Bartheloff*, 31.03.1945; and KLA, AT-KLA 39-C-18.1138, 18.1147, 18.1188, 18.1072, 18.1330, 18.1451, 18.1660.

Chapter 5

1. On the *Zollhund* and *Zollhundeführer*, see ARS, SI AS 1931, t.e. 806, t.e. 806, BZKom (G) Wocheiner-Feistritz, BZKom (G) Wocheiner-Feistritz, *Lagebericht März 1945*, 29.03.1945, and *Lagebericht April 1945*, 30.04.1945; ibid., SI AS 2175, t.e. 17, Der Generalgrenzinspektur-IV G 2 a, *Ausbildung von Zollhundführern und Zollhunden*, 30.10.1944; ibid., Vorsteher des HZA Villach, *Ausbildung von Zollhundeführern und Zollhunden in Monat Jänner 1944* (but probably 1945), 21.12.1944; ibid., BdS Salzburg–Der Grenzreferent, *Abschrift zur Kenntnis und Beachtung*, 22.12.1944; ibid., KdS Veldes–Abt. ZGSch. Oberkrain in Krainburg, senza titolo, 05.02.1945; BZKom (G) Wocheiner-Feistritz, *Wachhunde*, 07.02.1945; ibid., BZKom (G) Wocheiner-Feistritz, *Veränderungsanzeige; Abstellung zu Lehrgängen*, 07.03.1945; and KLA, AT-KLA 39-C-18.1454.

Chapter 6

1. On the war and service merit awards, see ARS, SI AS 2175, t.e. 17, BZKom (G) Laak-Süd, *Bandenkampfabzeichen*, 20.05 and 16.06.1944; ibid., BZKom (G), *Vorschlagsliste für die Verleihung des KvK II. Klasse mit Schwertern*, 08.12.1944; Rudolf Schaffer–Zollinspektor-BZKom (G) Wocheiner-Feistritz, *Verleihungsbestimmungen für das Bandenkampfabzeichen*, 23.01.1945; BZKom (G) Wocheiner-Feistritz, *Bandenkampfabzeichen*, 10.02.1945; ibid., GASt Zarz, *Vorschläge zur Verleihung des*

KvK 2. Kl. m. Schw., 13.03.1945; ibid., GASt Wocheiner-Feistritz-West, *Vorschläge für die Verleihung des KvK II. Kl m. Schw.*, 14.03.1945; ibid., GASt Petersberg, *Vorschläge zur Verleihung des KvK II. Kl. m. Schw.*, 14.03.1945; ibid., BZKom (G) Wocheiner-Feistritz, *Vorschlagsliste für die Verleihung des KvK. II. Kl. m. Schw.*, 15.03.1945; ibid., GASt Wocheiner-Feistritz, *Vorschläge von Anträgen zur Verleihung des KvK II. Kl m. Schw.*, 15.03.1945; ibid., KdS Veldes–Abt. ZGSch. Oberkrain in Krainburg, *Verleihung von KvK 2. Kl. m. Schw.*, 28.03.1945; BA, R 601/2433, Präsidialkanzlei, *Vorschlagsliste Nr. 220/42 für die Verleihung des Zollgrenzschutz-Ehrenzeichens*, 20.11.1942; ibid., R601/2462, Präsidialkanzlei, *Vorschlagsliste für die Verleihung des Zollgrenzschutz-Ehrenzeichens Nr. 4/40, 12/43, 20/43, and 42/43*, respectively dated 19.01.1940, 20.01, 10.02, and 10.03.1943; BA-MA, RH 7/1816, Oberkommando des Heeres, *Verleihungsliste für Verleihung des KvK 2. Kl. m. Schw.*, 30.01, 20.04, and 01.09.1942, and 30.01 and 01.09.1943, and Heerespersonalamt, *Verleihungsliste für Verleihung des KvK 1. Kl. m. Schw.*, 11.09.1944; KLA, AT-KLA 39-C-18.1144; and ÖNB, *Alpenländische Rundschau*, Jahrg. 20, Fl. 20, 15.05.1943, p. 1.

Chapter 7

1. On the previous service in other military corps, see ARAR, Formulare und verschiedene Begleitdokumente für Displaced Persons in Österreich, Signatur 169800, Docs 80798132-80798153 (Alois Ravnik); ARS, SI AS 2175, t.e. 17, BZKom (G) Wocheiner-Feistritz, *Vorschlagsliste zur Beförderung von ZGSch Reservisten zu Hilfszollassistenten*, 14.02.1945; KLA, AT-KLA 39-C-18.1065, 18.1091, 18.1428, 18.1541, 18.1574, 18.1575, 18.1660, 18.1689; ibid., AT-KLA 128-F-H 61, *An "Grünen Grenzen"—Denkwürdigkeiten aus der Dienstzeit im Zollgrenzschutz von Karl Pfister*; and ÖNB, *Salzburger Zeitung*, Jahrg. 2, Nr. 127, 10.05.1943, p. 3.

2. On the transfers to other military units, see ARS, SI AS 2175, t.e. 17, Leiter d. BefSt d. ZGSch. Villach, *HZAss Albert Sponfelder*, 13.12.1944; ibid., BZKom (G) Wocheiner-Feistritz, *Freigabe des Zollgrenzschutzreservisten Ruschka Leopold*, 15.12.1944; ibid., Leiter d. BefSt d. ZGSch. Villach, *Freigabe von Zollgrenzschutzangehörigen für den Rüstungsstab Kammler*, 21.12.1944; ibid., BZKom (G) Wocheiner-Feistritz, *Abordnung eines Schuhmachers*, 26.01.1945; ibid., Der Kompanieführer 1. Einsatzkompanie Donaueschingen-gez. Nelde, *Abschrift*, 26.01.1945; ibid., BdS Salzburg–Der Grenzreferent, *Mangelhafte Ausstattung der 1. Einsatzkompanie Donaueschingen*, 03.02.1945; ibid., GASt Wocheiner-Feistritz-West, *Meldung*, 13.02.1945; ibid., BZKom (G) Wocheiner-Feistritz, *Nachweisung*, 04.02.1945; ibid., BZKom (G) Wocheiner-Feistritz, *Mangelhafte Ausstattung der Eins.Kp.*, 14.02.1945; ibid., BZKom (G) Enderlein, *Niederschrift* in KdS Veldes–Abt. ZGSch. Oberkrain in Krainburg, *Abschrift zur Kenntnis*, 13.03.1945; ibid., KdS Veldes–Abt. ZGSch. Oberkrain in Krainburg, *HZBAss Winter Einberufung; Fernmündlich voraus*, 13.03.1945; ibid., BZKom (G) Wocheiner-Feistritz, *Anton Valentinisch*, 24.03.1945; ibid., BZKom (G) Wocheiner-Feistritz, *Hilfswillige*, 28.03.1945; BA, R 110 Anh./18, Einsatzgruppe Oberrhein; Deutsches Rotes Kreuz–Suchdienst München, Vermißtenbildliste (Munich: 1957), 346–349; KLA, AT-KLA 39-C-18.1529 and 18.1623; and Walter Eulitz, *Die Geschichte des Zollgrenzdienstes (Der Zollgrenzdienst)* (Bonn, Germany: Wilhelm Stollfuß Verlag, 1968), 232.

Chapter 8

1. On psychological implications, discipline, and military justice, see ARS, SI AS 1067/III, šk. 26, *Mrliška knjiga Kranjska Gora*; ibid., SI AS 2175, t.e. 17, RSHA–Der Generalgrenzinspekteur-IV G 3, *An alle Staatspolizei(leit)stellen und Kommandeure der Sipo/SD mit Grenze*, 06.01.1945; ibid., BdS Salzburg-Untersuchungsführer, *Unerlaubte Entfernung*, 17.02.1945; ibid., KdS Veldes–Abt. ZGSch. Oberkrain in Krainburg, *Trennungsentschädigung für HZAss T.*, 16.03.1945; ibid., KdS Veldes–Abt. ZGSch. Oberkrain in Krainburg, *Verhalten auf Streifen und Postierungen*, 18.03.1945; ibid., BZKom (G) Wocheiner-Feistritz, *Trennungsentschädigung für HZAss. Max T.*, 22.03.1945; ibid., SS-u. Polizeigericht XVIII–Zweigstelle Salzburg, *Anklageverfügung und Haftbefehl!*, 31.03.1945; BA, R 110 Anh./6, BdS im Generalgouvernement, *Unterstellung des Zollgrenzschutzes unter die SS- und die Polizeigerichtsbarkeit*, 02.11.1944; and KLA, AT-KLA 39-C-18.394, 18.1065, 18.1161, 18.1188, 18.1334, 18.1390, 18.1431, 18.1520, 18.1571, 18.1629, 18.1642, 18.1646.

Chapter 9

1. Some units of the Zollgrenzschutz of the HZA Villach, temporarily subordinated to the Wehrmacht, were deployed against the Royal Yugoslav Army during the very early stages of the invasion of Slovenia. No detailed information is known regarding this phase.

2. ARS, SI 1622, t.e. 19, Gendarmeriekreis Radmannsdorf, *Lagebericht vom 24. Dezember 1941*, 24.12.1941; and ibid., SI AS 1622/II, t.e. 34, Der Kommandeur der Gendarmerie Südkärnten, *Nachrichten über Vorkommnisse in Südkärnten*, 07.01.1942.

3. ARS, SI 1622, t.e. 19, Gendarmeriekreis Radmannsdorf, *Lagebericht für den Monat März 1942*, 24.03.1942.

4. ARS, SI AS 2175, t.e. 16, BdO-BefSt Veldes, *Lage am 23.7.1942*, 23.07.1942.

5. ARS, SI AS 2173, t.e. 48, Gendarmerieposten Kronau, *An den BdO Alpenland–BefSt Veldes*, 31.07.1942; and ibid., SI AS 2175, t.e. 16, BdO–BefSt Veldes-Ic, *Lage am 2.8.1942*, 02.08.1942.

6. ARS, SI AS 1622, t.e. 1, BdO Alpenland–BefSt Veldes-Ic, *Lage am 24.8.1942*, 24.08.1942.

7. ARS, SI AS 2175, t.e. 16, BdO BefSt Veldes, *Lage am 9.9.1942*, 09.09.1942.

8. ARS, SI AS 2175, t.e. 16, BdO BefSt Veldes, *Lage am 13.9.1942*, 13.09.1942.

9. ARS, SI AS 2175, t.e. 16, BdO BefSt Veldes, *Lage am 15.9.1942*, 15.09.1942.

10. Jože Dežman, *Gorenjski partizan—Gorenjski odred 1942–1944* (Kranj, Slovenia: 1992), 149.

11. Hilfszollassistent Gotthard Miggitsch, born in Malborgeth in 1898, was buried in Bohinjska Bistrica at a currently unknown place (probably at the World War I Austro-Hungarian military cemetery). On him, see ARS, SI AS 1067/III, t.e. 3, *Mrliška knjiga Bohinjska Bistrica*; ibid., SI AS 2175, t.e. 16, BdO–BefSt Veldes-Ic, *Lage am 1.12.1942*, 01.12.1942; BA, R 2/123179, *Amtsblatt der Reichsfinanzverwaltung*, Jahrg. 25, 04.03.1943, Nr. 9, p. 70; KLA, AT-KLA 39-C-18.1362; OeStA, AdR MilEv ZGS, personal file of Gotthard Miggitsch; and www.volksbund.de (wrong date of death).

12. ARS, SI AS 2175, t.e. 15, BdO Alpenland–BefSt Veldes-Ic, *Informationsdienst Nr. 14*, 12.05.1943.

13. ARS, SI AS 2175, t.e. 15, BdO Alpenland–BefSt Veldes-Ic, *Informationsdienst Nr. 22*, 05.06.1943. The operation was probably carried out as a consequence of the activity of the partisan units in the eastern part of the Bohinj basin (Kreis Radmannsdorf) and in the area of Sorica-Soriška Planina (Kreis Krainburg) during spring 1943. It is known, in fact, that on May 22, the partisans tried to ambush a *Zollassistent* in Spodnja Sorica; also, on May 28, they attacked the ZASt (G) Zarz, while, on May 30, they tried to occupy the "Zollstützpunkt Dautscha," which at the time were both still subordinated to HZA Krainburg. Furthermore, during the same period, six border guards belonging to the ZASt (G) Zarz were killed within the same area; they were Hilfszollbetriebsassistent Franz Langer and Alfred Tannert from the "Zollstützpunkt Zarz-Landstrasse" (killed on March 13, in the locality of Plašajtar, near the Reichsgrenze), Hilfszollbetriebsassistent Willi Frehsberg (killed on April 9, on Mount Tonderškofel, height 1322, "Moschitsch-Hütte"), Zollsekretär Erich Schomaker (killed on May 24, between Sorica and Podrošt), and Zollsekretär Georg Wimmer and Zollassistent Friedrich Korbmacher (both killed on May 28, between Sorica and Zgornje Danje). On their death and these episodes, see ARS, SI AS 2175, t.e. 15, BdO Alpenland–BefSt Veldes-Ic, *Lage am 15. März 1943*, 15.03.1943, and *Informationsdienst Nr. 3*, 10.04.1943, *Nr. 18*, 24.05.1943 and *Nr. 20*, 30.05.1943; ibid., AS II, Akcesija št. 301, *Nemško vojaško pokopališče Kranj*; BA, R 2/123179, *Amtsblatt der Reichsfinanzverwaltung*, Jahrg. 25, 23.08.1943, Nr. 30, p. 209 and Jahrg. 25, 18.11.1943, Nr. 39, p. 269; ibid., R 2/123180, *Amtsblatt der Reichsfinanzverwaltung*, Jahrg. 26, 10.01.1944, Nr. 1, p. 2; Jože Dežman, *Gorenjski partizan-Gorenjski odred 1942–1944* (Kranj, Slovenia: 1992), 112; OeStA, AdR MilEv ZGS, personal files of Willi Frehsberg and Alfred Tannert; and www.volksbund.de.

14. ARS, SI AS 2175, t.e. 15, BdO Alpenland–BefSt Veldes-Ic, *Informationsdienst Nr. 27*, 20.06.1943.

15. ARS, SI AS 2175, t.e. 15, BdO Alpenland–BefSt Veldes-Ic, *Informationsdienst Nr. 28*, 23.06.1943.

16. ARS, SI AS 2175, t.e. 15, BdO Alpenland–BefSt Veldes-Ic, *Informationsdienst Nr. 30*, 29.06.1943.

17. ARS, SI AS 1622, t.e. 19, Gendarmerieposten Lengenfeld, *Lagebericht von 13. Juli 1943*, 10.07.1943; ibid., SI AS 2175, t.e. 15, BdO Alpenland–BefSt Veldes-Ic, *Informationsdienst Nr. 31*, 02.07.1943; and Mile Pavlin, *Jeseniško Bohinjski Odred* (Ljubljana, Slovenia: Knjižnica NOV in POJ, 1970), 30.

18. ARS, SI AS 2175, t.e. 15, BdO Alpenland–BefSt Veldes-Ic, *Informationsdienst Nr. 32*, 05.07.1943; ibid., AS II, Akcesija št. 301, *Nemško vojaško pokopališče Kranj*; and Mile Pavlin, *Jeseniško Bohinjski Odred* (Ljubljana, Slovenia: Knjižnica NOV in POJ, 1970), 30.

19. ARS, SI AS 1622, t.e. 19, Gendarmerieposten Mitterdorf i. d. Wochein, *Lagebericht für Juni/Juli 1943*, 12.07.1943; and ibid., SI AS 2175, t.e. 15, BdO Alpenland–BefSt Veldes-Ic, *Informationsdienst Nr. 34*, 11.07.1943.

20. ARS, SI AS 2175, t.e. 15, BdO Alpenland–BefSt Veldes-Ic, *Informationsdienst Nr. 42*, 04.08.1943; ibid., t.e. 17, BdO Alpenland–BefSt Veldes, *Bericht über Grosseinsatz am Sairachberg vom 2. bis 4.8.1943*, 09.08.1943; ibid., AS II, Akcesija št. 301, *Nemško vojaško pokopališče Kranj*; and BA, R 20/142, SS-Pol.Rgt. 19 (6. Kp. and II. Btl.), *Einsatzbericht*, both dated 05.08.1943.

21. ARS, SI AS 1622, t.e. 19, BdO Alpenland–BefSt Veldes-Ia, *Einsatzbefehl Nr. 156*, 15.09.1943; and Gendarmeriekreis Radmannsdorf, *An den BdO Alpenland-BefSt in Veldes*, 16.09.1943.

22. Hilfszollbetriebsassistent Valentin Ruttnig, born in St. Ruprecht bei Klagenfurt in 1897, died of wounds at the Krankenhaus Gallenfels on 07.10.1943 and was buried at the German military cemetery of Kranj, Block III / Reihe 6 / Einzelgrab 5. On him and on this episode, see ARS, SI AS 1067, t.e. 31, *Mrliška knjiga Golnik*; ibid., SI AS 2175, t.e. 17, BZKom (G) Wocheiner-Feistritz, *Vorschlagsliste für die Verleihung des KvK II. Kl. m. Schw.*, 08.12.1944; ibid., AS II, Akcesija št. 301, *Nemško vojaško pokopališče Kranj*; BA, R 2/123180, *Amtsblatt der Reichsfinanzverwaltung*, Jahrg. 26, 23.03.1944, Nr. 13, p. 54; BA-MA, RH 7/1816, Oberkommando des Heeres, *Verleihungsliste für Verleihung des KvK 2. Kl. m. Schw.*, 01.09.1943; OeStA, AdR MilEv ZGS, personal file of Valentin Rutting; and www.volksbund.de.

23. Hilfszollbetriebsassistent Edmund Murhard, born in Bonn am Rhein in 1901, was buried at the German military cemetery of Kranj, Block III / Reihe 6 / Einzelgrab 8. On him, see ARS, SI AS 1067/III, t.e. 16, *Mrliška knjiga Bled/Gorje*; ibid., AS II, Akcesija št. 301, *Nemško vojaško pokopališče Kranj*; BA, Kartei der Verlust- und Grabmeldungen gefallener deutscher Soldaten 1939–1945 (via www.ancestry.de), B 563-2 Kartei / G-A 641/0937; ibid., R 2/123180, *Amtsblatt der Reichsfinanzverwaltung*, Jahrg. 26, 24.04.1944, Nr. 23, p. 98; OeStA, AdR MilEv ZGS, personal file of Edmund Murhard; and www.volksbund.de.

24. OeStA, AdR MilEv ZGS, personal file of Alois Gaugl.

25. ARS, SI 2175, t.e. 17, logbook with no title (BZKom [G] Laak-Süd?), entry III/20, 11-24.11.1943; ibid., GASt Schwarzenberg-Ost, *Meldung über den Einsatz der GASt Schwarzenberg-Ost vom 11.11–24.11.1943 auf Anordung des Herrn BZKom. Laak-Süd*, 05.12.1943 and the attachment with no heading, *Einsatz vom 11. November bis einschl. 22. Nov. 1943*, no date; and Stefano Di Giusto, *Operationszone Adriatisches Küstenland* (Udine, Italy: IFSML, 2005), 147–149.

26. Hilfszollbetriebsassistent Othmar Swozill, born in Knittelfeld in 1903, Erkennungsmarke "OFPräs Graz 1162," previously at the ZASt (G) Eisnern (HZA Krainburg), was buried at the military block of the Gorizia civilian cemetery, Block D / Reihe 1 / Einzelgrab 13. On him, see BA, Kartei der Verlust- und Grabmeldungen gefallener deutscher Soldaten 1939–1945 (via www.ancestry.de), B 563-2 Kartei / G-A 953/0054 (incorrectly indicated as fallen in "Santa Lucia"); ibid., R 2/123180, *Amtsblatt der Reichsfinanzverwaltung*, Jahrg. 26, 22.05.1944, Nr. 30, p. 126; BA-MA, RH 7/1816, Oberkommando des Heeres, *Verleihungsliste für Verleihung des KvK 2. Kl. m. Schw.*, 30.01.1943; Cimitero Civile di Gorizia, *Registro delle inumazioni dei militari tedeschi 1943–45*; KLA, AT-KLA 39-C-18.1645; and www.volksbund.de (listed as Swozil). On the operation, see ARS, SI AS 2175, t.e. 17, BZKom (G) Wocheiner-Feistritz, *Vorschlagsliste für die Verleihung des KvK II. Kl. m. Schw.*, 08.12.1944; ibid., GASt Petersberg, *Vorschläge zur Verleihung des KvK II. Kl. m. Schw.*, 14.03.1945; ibid., BZKom (G) Wocheiner-Feistritz, *Vorschlagsliste für die Verleihung des KvK. II. Kl. m. Schw.*, 15.03.1945; BA, Kartei der Verlust- und Grabmeldungen gefallener deutscher Soldaten 1939–1945 (via www.ancestry.de), B 563-2 Kartei / G-A 619/0755 and G-B 020/0434; and Stefano Di Giusto, *Operationszone Adriatisches Küstenland* (Udine, Italy: IFSML, 2005), 379.

27. Archive Košir, KdS Veldes, *Todesanzeige*, 03.02.1944; and Inštitut za zgodovino delavskega gibanja, *Zbornik* (Ljubljana, Slovenia: 1963), št. 208, 463.

28. Inštitut za zgodovino delavskega gibanja, *Zbornik* (Ljubljana, Slovenia: 1963), št. 219, 485.

29. Hilfszollbetriebsassistent Rudolf Rauter, born in Afritz bei Villach in 1914, was buried at the German military cemetery of Kranj, Block IV / Reihe 3 / Einzelgrab 15. On him, see ARS, AS II, Akcesija št. 301, *Nemško vojaško pokopališče Kranj*; BA, Kartei der Verlust- und Grabmeldungen gefallener deutscher Soldaten 1939–1945 (via www.ancestry.de), B 563-2 Kartei / G-A 747/0498; ibid., R 2/123180, *Amtsblatt der Reichsfinanzverwaltung*, Jahrg. 26, 25.07.1944, Nr. 37, p. 176; KLA, AT-KLA 39-C-18.1514; and www.volksbund.de. On this episode, see also ARS, SI AS 2175, t.e. 17, GASt Petersberg, *Vorschläge zur Verleihung des KvK II. Kl. m. Schw.*, 14.03.1945, and BZKom (G) Wocheiner-Feistritz, *Vorschlagsliste für die Verleihung des KvK. II. Kl. m. Schw.*, 15.03.1945; and OeStA, AdR MilEv ZGS, personal file of Rudolf Rauter.

30. Hilfszollbetriebsassistent Josef Filippi, born in Purgstall/ND in 1899, was buried at the German military cemetery of Kranj, Block IV / Reihe 8 / Einzelgrab 14. On him, see ARS, AS II, Akcesija št. 301, *Nemško vojaško pokopališče Kranj*; BA, R 2/123180, *Amtsblatt der Reichsfinanzverwaltung*, Jahrg. 26, 25.07.1944, Nr. 37, p. 174; KLA, AT-KLA 39-C-18.1112; OeStA, AdR MilEv ZGS, personal file of Josef Filippi; and www.volksbund.de. About Hilfszollbetriebsassistent Ernst Salfellner, born in Leoben in 1898, see ARS, ASII, Akcesija št. 301, *Nemško vojaško pokopališče Kranj*; BA, Kartei der Verlust- und Grabmeldungen gefallener deutscher Soldaten 1939–1945 (via www.ancestry.de), B 563-2 Kartei / G-A 138/0247; ibid., R 2/123180, *Amtsblatt der Reichsfinanzverwaltung*, Jahrg. 26, 05.08.1944, Nr. 38, p. 183; OeStA, AdR MilEv ZGS, personal file of Ernst Salfellner; and www.volksbund.de.

31. On Hilfszollbetriebsassistent Otto Max Schäfer, born in 1908, see OeStA, AdR MilEv ZGS, personal file of Otto Schäfer; and www.volksbund.de.

32. ARS, SI AS 2175, t.e. 17, 188. Res.Geb.Div. (v. Hösslin), *Abschrift!*, 19.04.1944; ibid., BZKom (G) (Wocheiner-Feistritz), *Vorschlagsliste für die Verleihung des KvK II. Kl. m. Schw.*, 08.12.1944; ibid., Rudolf Schaffer–Zollinspektor-BZKom (G) Wocheiner-Feistritz, *Verleihungsbestimmungen für das Bandenkampfabzeichen*, 23.01.1945; ibid., GASt Petersberg, *Vorschläge zur Verleihung des KvK II. Kl. m. Schw.*, 14.03.1945; and ibid., BZKom (G) Wocheiner-Feistritz, *Vorschlagsliste für die Verleihung des KvK. II. Kl. m. Schw.*, 15.03.1945.

33. ARS, SI AS 2175, t.e. 17, GASt Petersberg, *Vorschläge zur Verleihung des KvK II. Kl. m. Schw.*, 14.03.1945; and ibid., BZKom (G) Wocheiner-Feistritz, *Vorschlagsliste für die Verleihung des KvK. II. Kl. m. Schw.*, 15.03.1945.

34. Hilfszollsekretär Josef Spörk, born in Graz in 1895, Erkennungsmarke "Zollgrenzschutz Graz 784," previously Stützpunktführer Mitterdorf in Wochein, died the following day while being transported to the Krankenhaus Gallenfels and was later buried at the German military cemetery of Kranj, Block VI / Reihe 2 / Einzelgrab 3. On him, see ARS, SI AS 1067/III, t.e. 3, *Mrliška knjiga Srednja vas v Bohinju*; ibid., AS II, Akcesija št. 301, *Nemško vojaško pokopališče Kranj*; BA, Kartei der Verlust- und Grabmeldungen gefallener deutscher Soldaten 1939–1945 (via www.ancestry.de), B 563-2 Kartei / G-A

464/0597; ibid., R 2/123180, *Amtsblatt der Reichsfinanzverwaltung*, Jahrg. 26, 02.10.1944, Nr. 42, p. 215; KLA, AT-KLA 39-C-18.1629; and Stanko Petelin, *Gradnikova Brigada* (Ljubljana, Slovenia: Založba borec in revija Naša obramba, 1983), 375–376.

35. Hilfszollbetriebsassistent Thomas Linder, born in Gurk in 1904, Erkennungsmarke "OFPräs Graz 585," was buried at the German military cemetery of Kranj, Block VI / Reihe 3 / Einzelgrab 7. On him, see ARS, SI AS 1067/III, t.e. 3, *Mrliška knjiga Bohinjska Bistrica*; ibid., AS II, Akcesija št. 301, *Nemško vojaško pokopališče Kranj*; BA, Kartei der Verlust- und Grabmeldungen gefallener deutscher Soldaten 1939–1945 (via www.ancestry.de), B 563-2 Kartei / G-A 783/0945; ibid., R 2/123180, *Amtsblatt der Reichsfinanzverwaltung*, Jahrg. 26, 02.10.1944, Nr. 42, p. 213; KLA, AT-KLA 39-C-18.1319; and OeStA, AdR MilEv ZGS, personal file of Thomas Linder. On the attack, see Stanko Petelin, *Gradnikova Brigada* (Ljubljana, Slovenia: Založba borec in revija Naša obramba, 1983), 385–386.

36. Zollsekretär Heinrich Kreuz, born in München in 1906, was buried at an unknown place. On him, see ARS, SI AS 1067/III, t.e. 3, *Mrliška knjiga Bohinjska Bistrica*; BA, R 601/2462, Präsidialkanzlei, *Vorschlagsliste Nr. 20/43 für die Verleihung des Zollgrenzschutz-Ehrenzeichens*, 10.02.1943; and BA-MA, RH 7/1816, Oberkommando des Heeres, *Verleihungsliste für Verleihung des KvK 2. Kl. m. Schw.*, 01.09.1943.

37. ARS, SI AS 1618, t.e. 1, HSSPF im Wehrkreis XVIII-FSBB, *Lage*, 01.07.1944; and Inštitut za zgodovino delavskega gibanja, *Zbornik* (Ljubljana, Slovenia: 1972), št. 144, 634.

38. Zollsekretär Fritz Hartwich, born in Gutweinen (Kreis Darkehmen) in 1904, Erkennungsmarke "OFPräs Königsberg 758," was buried at the German military cemetery of Kranj, Block VI / Reihe 6 / Einzelgrab 6. On him, see ARS, SI AS 1067/III, t.e. 3, *Mrliška knjiga Bohinjska Bistrica*; ibid., AS II, Akcesija št. 301, *Nemško vojaško pokopališče Kranj*; BA, Kartei der Verlust- und Grabmeldungen gefallener deutscher Soldaten 1939–1945 (via www.ancestry.de), B 563-2 Kartei / G-B 036/0570; ibid., R 2/123180, *Amtsblatt der Reichsfinanzverwaltung*, Jahrg. 26, 11.12.1944, Nr. 45, p. 238 (incorrectly indicated as in force at the ZASt (G) Schmalleningken at the time of death); and www.volksbund.de. Hilfszollbetriebsassistent Wilhelm Dannehl, born in Munich/Gladbach in 1904, Erkennungsmarke "OFPräs Westmark 1654" (removed by the partisans), was buried at the German military cemetery of Kranj, Block VI / Reihe 6 / Einzelgrab 7. On him, see ARS, AS II, Akcesija št. 301, *Nemško vojaško pokopališče Kranj*; BA, Kartei der Verlust- und Grabmeldungen gefallener deutscher Soldaten 1939–1945 (via www.ancestry.de), B 563-2 Kartei / G-B 239/0716; ibid., R 2/123180, *Amtsblatt der Reichsfinanzverwaltung*, Jahrg. 26, 20.11.1944, Nr. 44, p. 228; and OeStA, AdR MilEv ZGS, personal file of Wilhelm Dannehl. On Hilfszollbetriebsassistent Josef Prazdny, born in Vienna in 1907, Erkennungsmarke "OFPräs Graz 779," see Innerhofer Archive, Gendarmerie-Hochgebirgsposten Wocheiner-Feistritz, *Nachtragsmeldung zur Bandenmeldung*, 30.06.1944 (in copy); and KLA, AT-KLA 39-C-18.1488.

39. ARS, SI AS 1618, t.e. 1, HSSPF im Wehrkreis XVIII-FSBB, *Lage*, 01.07 and 02.07.1944; ibid., SI AS 2175, t.e. 17, Rudolf Schaffer–Zollinspektor-BZKom (G) Wocheiner-Feistritz, *Verleihungsbestimmungen für das Bandenkampfabzeichen*, 23.01.1945; ibid., GASt Petersberg, *Vorschläge zur Verleihung des KvK II. Kl. m. Schw.*, 14.03.1945;

BZKom (G) Wocheiner-Feistritz, *Vorschlagsliste für die Verleihung des KvK. II. Kl. m. Schw.*, 15.03.1945; ibid., AS II, Akcesija št. 301, *Nemško vojaško pokopališče Kranj*; BA, Kartei der Verlust- und Grabmeldungen gefallener deutscher Soldaten 1939–1945 (via www.ancestry.de), B 563-2 Kartei / G-A 007/0518, 420/2108 and 848/0358; Stefano Di Giusto, *Operationszone Adriatisches Küstenland* (Udine, Italy: IFSML, 2005), 511–513; and Stanko Petelin, *Gradnikova Brigada* (Ljubljana, Slovenia: Založba borec in revija Naša obramba, 1983), 417–439.

40. ARS, SI AS 1618, t.e. 1, HSSPF im Wehrkreis XVIII-FSBB, *Lage*, 07.07.1944.; and ibid., SI AS 2175, t.e. 17, BZKom (G) Wocheiner-Feistritz, *Vorschlagsliste für die Verleihung des KvK II. Kl. m. Schw.*, 08.12.1944.

41. OeStA, AdR MilEv ZGS, personal file of Johann Schanig.

42. KLA, AT-KLA 522-8, folder 10, *Tägliche Lageberichte des Kommandeurs der Gendarmerie beim Reichsstatthalter in Kärnten*, 27.08.1944.

43. Hilfszollassistent Peter Gössler, born in Hirschegg/Rain in 1904, indicated as "Im Einsatz gegen Banditen gefallen," was buried at a currently unknown place. On him, see OeStA, AdR MilEv ZGS, personal file of Peter Gössler.

44. ARS, SI AS 2175, t.e. 17, BZKom (G) (Wocheiner-Feistritz), *Vorschlagsliste für die Verleihung des KvK II. Kl. m. Schw.*, 08.12.1944; and ibid., GASt Wocheiner-Feistritz, *Vorschläge von Anträgen zur Verleihung des KvK II. Kl m. Schw.*, 15.03.1945.

45. ARS, SI AS 1622, t.e. 19, Gendarmerieposten Kronau, *Bandenmeldung Nr. 17/44*, 21.09.1944.

46. KLA, AT-KLA 522-8, folder 10, *Tägliche Lageberichte des Kommandeurs der Gendarmerie beim Reichsstatthalter in Kärnten*, 14.10.1944.

47. Hilfszollassistent Adolf Preiß, born in Leisuhnen (Kreis Heiligenbeil) in 1902, reported as "gefallen in Bandenkampf," was buried at the "Heldenfriedhof Wocheiner-Feistritz" (most likely the World War I Austro-Hungarian military cemetery in Bohinjska Bistrica). On him and on this episode, see ARS, SI AS 1067/III, t.e. 3, *Mrliška knjiga Bohinjska Bistrica*; ibid., SI AS 2175, t.e. 17, BZKom (G) Wocheiner-Feistritz, *Vorschlagsliste für die Verleihung des KvK II. Kl. m. Schw.*, 08.12.1944; Mile Pavlin, *Jeseniško Bohinjski Odred* (Ljubljana, Slovenia: Knjižnica NOV in POJ, 1970), 110–111; OeStA, AdR MilEv ZGS, personal file of Adolf Preiss; and www.volksbund.de.

48. ARS, SI AS 2175, t.e. 17, GASt Zarz, *Vorschläge zur Verleihung des KvK II. Kl. m. Schw.*, 13.03.1945; and ibid., BZKom (G) Wocheiner-Feistritz, *Vorschlagsliste für die Verleihung des KvK. II. Kl. m. Schw.*, 15.03.1945.

49. ARS, SI AS 1622, t.e. 19, Gendarmerieposten Kronau, *Bandenmeldung Nr. 29/44*, 02.11.1944.

50. Hilfszollassistent Georg Laber, born in Pöllan bei Villach in 1900, was buried in Feistritz an der Drau. On him, see ARS, SI AS 1067/III, šk. 26, *Mrliška knjiga Kranjska Gora*; KLA, AT-KLA 39-C-18.1301; ibid., AT-KLA 128-F-H 61, *An "Grünen Grenzen"—Denkwürdigkeiten aus der Dienstzeit im Zollgrenzschutz von Karl Pfister*; and OeStA, AdR MilEv ZGS, personal file of Georg Laber.

51. KLA, AT-KLA 522-8, folder 10, *Tägliche Lageberichte des Kommandeur der Gendarmerie beim Reichsstatthalter in Kärnten*, 10.11.1944.

52. ARS, SI AS 1622, t.e. 19, Gendarmerieposten Kronau, *Bandenmeldung Nr. 29/44*, 02.11.1944, Gendarmerie-Hochgebirgsposten Wocheiner-Feistritz, *Bandenmeldung Nr. 70/44*, 13.11.1944, and *An den KdS in Veldes*, 16.11.1944; ibid., SI AS 2175, t.e. 17, BZKom (G) (Wocheiner-Feistritz), *Vorschlagsliste für die Verleihung des KvK II. Kl. m. Schw.*, 08.12.1944; KLA, AT-KLA 128-F-H 61, *An "Grünen Grenzen"—Denkwürdigkeiten aus der Dienstzeit im Zollgrenzschutz von Karl Pfister*; Inštitut za zgodovino delavskega gibanja, *Zbornik* (Ljubljana, Slovenia: 1986), št. 129, 860; and Mile Pavlin, *Jeseniško Bohinjski Odred* (Ljubljana, Slovenia: Knjižnica NOV in POJ, 1970), 95–98 and 128–132.

53. Zollsekretär Max Exner, born in Waldneudorf in 1903, was buried at an unknown place in the locality of "Feistritz–Slowenien." Hilfszollassistent Johann Paulitsch was buried at the German military cemetery of Kranj at the Block VII / Reihe 3 / Einzelgrab 12, and his name appears on the war memorial of Globasnitz in Carinthia. On their death and on this story, see ARS, SI AS 2175, t.e. 17, Vorsteher des HZA Villach, *Abschrift!*, 25.10.1944; ibid., BZKom (G) Wocheiner-Feistritz, *Ausbildungslehrgänge*, 01.03.1945; ibid., AS II, Akcesija št. 301, *Nemško vojaško pokopališče Kranj*; OeStA, AdR MilEv ZGS, personal file of Oskar Gaeble; and www.volksbund.de.

54. Zollsekretär Heinrich Ibler, born in Etterzhausen in 1906, was buried at the German military cemetery of Sankt Veit an der Glan, grave 12/719. On him and on this episode, see Goris Archive, death card of Zollsekretär Ibler (in copy); ARS, SI AS 2175, t.e. 17, BdS Salzburg–Der Grenzreferent, *Abschrift zur Kenntnis und Beachtung*, 22.12.1944; BA-MA, RH 7/1816, Oberkommando des Heeres, *Verleihungsliste für Verleihung des KvK 2. Kl. m. Schw.*, 30.01.1943; KLA, AT-KLA 128-F-H 61, *An "Grünen Grenzen"—Denkwürdigkeiten aus der Dienstzeit im Zollgrenzschutz von Karl Pfister*; ÖNB, *Alpenländische Rundschau*, Jahrg. 24, Fl. 5, 23.12.1944, p. 3, and *Kärntner Volkszeitung*, Jahrg. 15, Fl. 146, 11.12.1944, p. 4; and www.volksbund.de.

55. ARS, SI AS 2175, t.e. 17, BZKom (G) Laak-West, *Bandenlage*, 21.11.1944; and ibid., Leiter d. BefSt d. ZGSch. Villach, *Anerkennung*, 18.12.1944 (two different documents).

56. KLA, AT-KLA 522-8, folder 10, *Tägliche Lageberichte des Kommandeurs der Gendarmerie beim Reichsstatthalter in Kärnten*, 30.11.1944.

57. ARS, SI AS 1622, t.e. 19, Gendarmerie-Hochgebirgsposten Wocheiner-Feistritz, *Bandenmeldung Nr. 78/44*, 08.12.1944 (in this report, the BZKom (G) Kasischke is incorrectly referred to as "Stützpunktkommandanten Bez. Zollkommissar Kraschinky"); ibid., SI AS 2175, t.e. 17, BZKom (G) Wocheiner-Feistritz, *Vorschlagsliste für die Verleihung des KvK II. Kl. m. Schw.*, 08.12.1944; ibid., BZKom (G) Wocheiner-Feistritz, *Vorschlagsliste für die Verleihung des KvK. II. Kl. m. Schw.*, 15.03.1945; ibid., GASt Wocheiner-Feistritz, *Vorschläge von Anträgen zur Verleihung des KvK II. Kl m. Schw.*, 15.03.1945; and Mile Pavlin, *Jeseniško Bohinjski Odred* (Ljubljana, Slovenia: Knjižnica NOV in POJ, 1970), 149–153.

58. KLA, AT-KLA 522-8, folder 10, *Tägliche Lageberichte des Kommandeurs der Gendarmerie beim Reichsstatthalter in Kärnten*, 08 and 14.12.1944.

59. ARS, SI AS 1622, t.e. 19, Gendarmerie-Hochgebirgsposten Wocheiner-Feistritz, *Bandenmeldung Nr. 82/44*, 14.12.1944.

60. ARS, SI AS 1622, t.e. 19, Gendarmerie-Hochgebirgsposten Legenfeld, *Bandenmeldung Nr. 92/44*, 19.12.1944.

61. Hilfszollassistent Alois Ferstl (born in Semriach in 1904), Julius Lassmann (born in Cilli in 1904), Paul Pfeifer (born in Zeitz in 1903), and Willi Rehe (born in Neustadt in 1904), all belonging to the Abteilung Zollgrenzschutz Oberkrain in Krainburg, were buried at the German military cemetery of Kranj, respectively to the Block VII / Reihe 6 / Einzelgrab 16, VII/6/18, VII/6/17, and VII/6/19. On them, see ARS, AS II, Akcesija št. 301, *Nemško vojaško pokopališče Kranj*; OeStA, AdR MilEv ZGS, personal files of Alois Ferstl, Julius Lassmann, Paul Pfeifer, and Willi Rehe; and www.volksbund.de. On this episode, see ARS, SI AS 2175, t.e. 17, GASt Wocheiner-Feistritz-West, *Vorschläge für die Verleihung des KvK II. Kl m. Schw.*, 14.03.1945; ibid., BZKom (G) Wocheiner-Feistritz, *Vorschlagsliste für die Verleihung des KvK. II. Kl. m. Schw.*, 15.03.1945; ibid., BZKom (G) Wocheiner-Feistritz, *Verwundetenabzeichen*, 20.03.1945; Mile Pavlin, *Jeseniško Bohinjski Odred* (Ljubljana, Slovenia: Knjižnica NOV in POJ, 1970), 206–207; and OeStA, AdR MilEv ZGS, personal file of Hermann Schirmer.

62. ARS, SI AS 1931, t.e. 806, BZKom (G) Wocheiner-Feistritz, *Lagebericht März 1945*, 29.03.1945; and Mile Pavlin, *Jeseniško Bohinjski Odred* (Ljubljana, Slovenia: Knjižnica NOV in POJ, 1970), 216–217.

63. ARS, SI AS 1931, t.e. 806, BZKom (G) Wocheiner-Feistritz, *Lagebericht März 1945*, 29.03.1945; ibid., SI AS 2175, t.e. 17, GASt Zarz, *Vorschläge zur Verleihung des KvK II. Kl. m. Schw.*, 13.03.1945; ibid., GASt Petersberg, *Vorschläge zur Verleihung des KvK II. Kl. m. Schw.*, 14.03.1945; ibid., BZKom (G) Wocheiner-Feistritz, *Vorschlagsliste für die Verleihung des KvK. II. Kl. m. Schw.*, 15.03.1945; and ibid., BZKom (G) Wocheiner-Feistritz, *Verwundetenabzeichen*, 20.03.1945.

64. ARS, SI AS 1931, t.e. 806, BZKom (G) Wocheiner-Feistritz, *Lagebericht März 1945*, 29.03.1945.

65. ARS, SI AS 1931, t.e. 761, no heading, *Einsatzplan für den 4.4.1945*, no date; ibid., t.e. 806, BZKom (G) Wocheiner-Feistritz, *Lagebericht März 1945*, 29.03.1945, and *Lagebericht April 1945*, 30.04.1945; ibid., BZKom (G) Wocheiner-Feistritz, *Bandenbewegungen seit dem Pol. Einsatz (20.3.45) im Raume Petersberg–Zarz–Kirchheim*, 04.04.1945; ibid., BZKom (G) Wocheiner-Feistritz, *Tätigkeitsbericht*, 06.04.1945; ibid., BZKom (G) Wocheiner-Feistritz, *Bandenbewegung nach dem Polizeieinsatz*, 14.04.1945; Mile Pavlin, *Jeseniško Bohinjski Odred* (Ljubljana, Slovenia: Knjižnica NOV in POJ, 1970), 230–235 and 245–249; and Radosav Isaković-Rade, *Kosovelova Brigada* (Ljubljana, Slovenia: Knjižnica NOV in POJ, 1973), 647–717.

Chapter 10

1. Sources used for the chapter about the last weeks of war are ARS, SI AS 1931, t.e. 806, BZKom (G) Wocheiner-Feistritz, *Lagebericht März 1945*, 29.03.1945, and *Lagebericht April 1945*, 30.04.1945; ibid., BZKom (G) Wocheiner-Feistritz, *Tätigkeitsbericht*, 13.04.1945; ibid., BZKom (G) Wocheiner-Feistritz, *Bandenbewegung nach dem Polizeieinsatz*, 14.04.1945; KLA, AT-KLA 128-F-H 61, *An "Grünen Grenzen"—Denkwürdigkeiten aus der Dienstzeit im Zollgrenzschutz von Karl Pfister*.

2. Apparently missing while on duty in the area of Bohinjska Bistrica (Kreis Radmannsdorf) in May 1945 was also Zollassistent Josef Markoutz, born in Austria in 1904, on whom it was not possible to find further information. On him, see Deutsches Rotes Kreuz-Suchdienst München, *Vermißtenbildliste* (Munich: 1957), 479; and ÖNB, *Volkswille*, Jahrg. 1, Nr. 67, 01.06.1946, p. 4.

Bibliography and Sources

Archives

ARAR (Arolsen Archives, Bad Arolsen, Germany)

ARS (Arhiv Republike Slovenije, Ljubljana, Slovenia)

ASU (Archivio di Stato, Udine, Italy)

ASV (Archivio di Stato, Varese, Italy)

BA (Bundesarchiv, Berlin-Lichterfelde, Germany)

BA-MA (Bundesarchiv Militärarchiv, Freiburg im Breisgau, Germany)

INZ (Inštitut za novejšo zgodovino, Ljubljana, Slovenia)

KLA (Kärntner Landesarchiv, Klagenfurt, Austria)

NARA (National Archives and Records Administration, Washington, DC)

OeStA (Österreichisches Staatsarchiv, Vienna)

ÖNB (Österreichischen Nationalbibliothek, Vienna)

ZAL-ŠKL (Zgodovinski Arhiv Ljubljana—Enota v Škofji Loki, Škofja Loka, Slovenia)

Selected Bibliography

Adami, Vittorio (per il Ministero della Guerra, Stato Maggiore Del Regio Esercito, Ufficio Storico). *Storia documentata dei Confini del Regno d'Italia*. Vol. IV, *Confine Italo-Jugoslavo*. Rome: Istituto Poligrafico dello Stato, 1931.

Buchheim, Hans. *SS und Polizei im NS-Staat*. Vol. 13 of the *Staatspolitische Schriftenreihe* (Sammlung über Recht des Nationalsozialismus). Duisdorf, Germany: Studiengesellschaft für Zeitprobleme, 1964.

Cafuta, Darko, Jože Dežman, and Marcus Schreiner Božič. *Deutsche und Partisanen, Deutsche Verluste in Gorenjska (Oberkrain) zwischen Mythos und Wahrheit*. Kranj, Slovenia: Gorenjski Muzej, 2016.

Deutsches Rotes Kreuz—Suchdienst München. *Vermißtenbildliste*. Vol. II GH. Munich: 1957.

Dežman, Jože. *Gorenjski partizan—Gorenjski odred 1942–1944*. Kranj, Slovenia: 1992.

Di Bartolomeo, Michele, and Federico Sancimino. *Dal primo colpo all'ultima frontiera: La Guardia di Finanza a Gorizia e provincia; Una storia lunga un secolo*. Gorizia, Italy: LEG Edizioni, 2014.

Di Giusto, Stefano. *Operationszone Adriatisches Küstenland*. Udine, Italy: IFSML, 2005.

Državni Sekretarijat za unutrašnje poslove FNRJ. *Nemačka Obaveštajna Služba*. Vol. III. Belgrade, Yugoslavia: 1957.

Eulitz, Walter. *Die Geschichte des Zollgrenzdienstes (Der Zollgrenzdienst)*. Vol. 6 of the *Schriftenreihe des Bundesministeriums der Finanzen*. Bonn, Germany: Wilhelm Stollfuß Verlag, 1968.

Ferenc, Tone. *Nacistična raznarodovalna politika v Sloveniji v letih 1941–1945*. Maribor, Slovenia: 1968.

Ferenc, Tone. "Okupacijski sistemi med drugo svetovno vojno 1." In *Historia*. Oddelka za zgodovino Filosofske fakultete Univerze v Ljubljani, Nr. 12. Ljubljana, Slovenia: 2006.

Inštitut za Zgodovino Delavskega Gibanja. *Zbornik*. Part VI, *Borbe v Sloveniji 1944*. Knjiga 10, 14, and 17. Ljubljana, Slovenia: respectively 1963, 1972, and 1986.

Groth, Karl. *Der Reichsfinanzverwaltung*. Auflage 7 and 8 of the *Bücherei des Steuerrechts Band 1*. Berlin and Vienna: Industrieverlag Spaeth & Linde, 1942 and 1944.

Isakovič-Rade, Radosav. *Kosovelova Brigada*. Ljubljana, Slovenia: Knjižnica NOV in POJ, Partizanska knjiga, 1973.

Kocjančič, Klemen. "Bled v času nemške okupacije med drugo svetovno vojno (1941–1945)." In *Kronika*. Zveza zgodovinskih društev Slovenije 69, Nr. 2. Ljubljana, Slovenia: Fotolito Dolenc, 2021.

Linasi, Marian. *Die Kärntner Partisanen*. Klagenfurt, Austria: Mohorjeva/Hermagoras, 2010.

Marktgemeinde Arnoldstein. *Zoll und Grenze(n): Die Geschichte des Zolls*. PDF file supplied by the municipality of Arnoldstein, Austria.

Mikša, Peter, and Matija Zorn. "Rapalska meja: Četrt stoletja obstoja in stoletje dediščine." In *Historia*. Oddelka za zgodovino Filosofske fakultete Univerze v Ljubljani, Nr. 25. Ljubljana, Slovenia: 2018.

Oberfinanzpräsidium Graz. *Durchführungsbestimmungen des Oberfinanzpräsidenten Graz zur Dienstordnung für die Oberfinanzpräsidenten*. 1944.

Pavlin, Mile. *Jeseniško Bohinjski Odred*. Ljubljana, Slovenia: Knjižnica NOV in POJ, Partizanska knjiga, 1970.

Petelin, Stanko. *Gradnikova Brigada*. Ljubljana, Slovenia: Založba borec in revija Naša obramba, 1983.

Rausch, Josef. *Der Partisanenkampf in Kärnten im Zweiten Weltkrieg*. Vol. 39/40 of the *Militärhistorische Schriftenreihe*. Vienna: ÖBV, 1994.

Reichsfinanzministerium (Herausgegeben im). *Dienstanweisung für die Zollabfertigung (ZAbfDA)*. Berlin: Gedruckt in der Reichsdruckerei, 1933.

Sandkühler, Thomas. "Von der 'Gegnerabwehr' zum Judenmord: Grenzpolizei und Zollgrenzschutz im NS-Staat." In *"Durchschnittstäter"—Handeln und Motivation*. Beiträge zur Geschichte des Nationalsozialismus 16. Assoziation Schwarze Risse–Rote Straße, 2000.

Schätz, Jos. Jul. (Geleitet von). *Zeitschrift des Deutschen und Österreichischen Alpenvereins*. Vol. 73, *Jahrgang 1942*. Munich: Verlag F. Bruckmann, 1942.

Società Alpina delle Giulie, Sezione di Trieste del Club Alpino Italiano. *Il Confine orientale d'Italia dalle Alpi Carniche al mare*. Trieste, Italy: Stabilimento Artistico Tipografico G. Caprin, 1920.

Supreme Headquarters Allied Expeditionary Forces–Evaluation and Dissemination Section, G-2 (Counter Intelligence Subdivision). *The German Police*. London: prepared jointly by M.I.R.S. (London Branch) and E.D.S. in consultation with the War Office (M.I. 14[d]), 1945.

Zoepfl, Dr. Gustav. *Kärnten: Ein Reisenhandbuch herausgegeben vom "Landesverband für Fremdenverkehr in Kärnten" und vom "Kärntnerverein."* Klagenfurt, Austria: Ferdinand v. Kleinmayr, 1906.

Walzl, August. *"Als erster Gau…": Entwicklungen und Strukturen des Nationalsozialismus in Kärnten*. Klagenfurt, Austria: Universitätsverlag Carinthia, 1992.

Magazines, Newspapers, and Periodic Bulletins

Adressbuch der Stadt Graz, 1943–1944

Alpenländische Rundschau, 1941–1943

Amtsblatt der Reichsfinanzverwaltung, 1941–1944

Der Gebirgsfreund, 1941

Kärntner Volkszeitung, 1939–1944

Innsbrucker Nachrichten, 1942–1944

Ostmark-Jahrbuch, 1941–1942

Salzburger Volksblatt, 1939

Salzburger Zeitung, 1943

Verordnungs- und Amtsblatt des Chefs der Zivilverwaltung für die/in den besetzten Gebieten Kärntens und Krains, 1941–1945

Maps

Karte der Alpen- und Donau-Reichsgaue

Maßstab 1:500000, Hauptvermessungsabteilung XIV Wien, Ausgabe IV. 1943.

Reichsgaue Wien, Niederdonau, Oberdonau, Salzburg, Tirol mit Vorlarlberg, Kärnten und Steiermark.

Maßstab 1:50000, Herausgegeben von Herausgegeben von OKH/Gen. St. d. H. 1944.

Arnoldstein, Blatt Nr. 5351/Ost; Hermagor, Blatt Nr. 5341/West; Krainburg, Blatt Nr. 5553/West; Zarz, Blatt Nr. 5552/West.

Deutsche Heereskarten

Jugoslawien 1:25000, Herausgegeben von OKH/Gen. St. d. H. 1943.

Bled (Veldes), Blatt Nr. 10-1-c, 10-1-d, 10-3-b; Tolmin (Tolmein), Blatt Nr. 9-2-a, 9-2-b, 9-2-d, 9-4-b.

UK Military Maps

Italy 1:25000, War Office, Geographical Section, General Staff, 1943 (IGM 1926).

Fusine in Valromana, Sheet 14a III N.E.; Strajaves (Hohenthurn), Sheet 14a IV S.E.; Passo Bogatin, Sheet 26 I N.W.

Websites

www.ancestry.de

www.arolsen-archives.org

www.etno-muzej.si

www.denkmalprojekt.org

www.rapalskameja.si

www.recherche-dienste.de

www.zollgrenzschutz.de

www.znaci.net

www.volksbund.de

Index

Personnel

Other units and offices